D0759083

The Art of
Moderation
An Alternative to Alcoholism

The Art of
Moderation
An Alternative to Alcoholism

John Michael

Vision Books International
Mill Valley, California

Library of Congress Card Number: 99-071333

Cover photography: Robert Brekke.
Book and cover design: Robert Brekke,
Publishers Design Group.

ISBN: 1-56550-083-0 (Hard Case)
ISBN: 1-56550-084-9 (Soft Cover)

Published by Vision Books International
Mill Valley, California 94941
415.451.7188

Printed in U.S.A.

Acknowledgments

There are several sources of information that contributed to my ability to recover from alcoholism and led to my writing this book. I listened to success tapes, read numerous books on diet and nutrition, and various self-help books, as well as spiritual/religious books.

Specifically, I would like to thank Brian Tracy and Anthony Robbins for their contemporary contribution to modern, positive psychology. I would also like to thank Pat Hardman for his concerns and input as a rehabilitating alcoholic; Dennis Attar and Murray Borod for their support during periods of time when I was a non-practicing alcoholic; Carol Rivendell, Kevin Kerwin, Gwen Cauthren, Kerri Mulligan, Michael Price, and Davoe Price for their interest and feedback on earlier versions of this book; Meg Stemper for her efforts in editing; and Sharon Jones for her patience and contribution of editing and publishing this book.

Dedication

I would like to dedicate this effort to my sister Carol, who for years supported me with her unconditional love, and emotional and financial support through the hardest times of my life. Not being able to adequately communicate to Carol the essence of my moderate lifestyle, following years of alcoholism, motivated me to record the substance of my now being a moderate person.

Introduction

I have avoided dialogue regarding my post-alcoholic moderation, but no longer wish to remain silent. I will bring to light and articulate, as best I can, a position of fact: I used to be an alcoholic and now I am not. Now I am a moderate person who drinks alcohol moderately, and I would like to share with you how I do it.

To those unaware of the nature of alcohol addiction and its subculture, there are practicing alcoholics and non-practicing alcoholics. Non-practicing alcoholics are those who abstain from alcohol but still think of themselves as alcoholics because they know if they were to drink alcohol at all, they would go right back to drinking uncontrollably (alcoholically). The statement "I used to be an alcoholic" is an impossible statement for them. Truer to fact is the statement, "Once an alcoholic, always an alcoholic" (*Alcoholics Anonymous* 33). This popular view allows no exceptions; if you discover you drink alcohol uncontrollably, it is a disposition that comes from your genes and you have no control over it. Therefore, based on this premise, your only alternatives are to be a practicing alcoholic or a non-practicing alcoholic, both having their associated sufferings and consequences.

It is my intention to demonstrate that, although some alcoholics may never be able to drink moderately, the pretense that *all* alcoholics are unable to rehabilitate themselves and be moderate drinkers is inaccurate.

To the individual who has never been inclined to abuse

alcohol, the psychological and behavioral suggestions contained in this book might seem too extreme and overstated, or too simplistic and obvious. It could also seem incomprehensible that any person would be able to be so abusive and self destructive. However, though it is not without conflict or denial while they're straight (sober), while intoxicated, alcoholics will have the illusion that everything is good (sometimes *very* good) and this euphoric experience will take precedence over everything else, becoming sought after and appreciated to the exclusion of amenable values. Alcoholics are inclined to "take it to the limit;" they need to see how far they can go with intoxication, thus exhibiting very extreme behavior. Consequently, the return to "normal" after exaggerated behavior like periodic intoxication requires compensation in psychology and behavior modification that might seem like extreme measures.

This book addresses the abusive behavior of the unquestionable alcoholic. To emphasize certain ideas, there will be some redundancy; that is, concepts will be reiterated so they cannot be missed. I will start with reiteration now and say, contrary to what might be perceived later in this book, these words are written primarily for the full-blown alcoholic. It is written from the perspective of an *ex-alcoholic* (one who *used* to drink alcohol uncontrollably on a regular basis). Though this writing is concerned with the apparent alcoholic, it also addresses the occasional drunk or the happy drunk: a large population of people who occasionally just want to have fun and use alcohol as a means to that end. Not all occasional, overindulgent drinkers become full-blown alcoholics; but, all alcoholics start off as occasional, overindulgent drinkers just having fun.

I remember that in the early stages of my alcoholic behavior, the desire for alternatives was quite prevalent, with the sickly experience of hangovers providing plenty of incentive for rehabilitation, but I found no tangible alternatives – programs or counseling – that provided anything other than total abstinence as a solution. In retrospect I realize that I, as well as others, enjoy alcohol and have an association with alcohol with an assortment of social events with family, friends, or work, so the motivation or desire to be totally abstinent is zilch. The individual who periodically suffers from hangovers will view abstinence as more intolerable than the occasional problems associated with overindulgence; so, the maturing alcoholic succumbs to abstinence only after the shame and remorse are greater than the pleasure of intoxication and/or the pleasure of social contacts involving alcohol. This is referred to as the necessary event of "hitting bottom."

It is my intention to provide alternatives in psychology and behavior that will enable the individual who suffers from overindulgence to avoid hitting bottom. This is where the occasional overindulgent drinker can recognize in themselves the symptoms of a developing problem and avoid the disaster of full-blown alcoholism before the "hitting a brick wall" approach, where everything changes. Individuals attempting total abstinence are prone to alienation and depression, with conflicts of willpower and identity. As an alternative, moderation can be seen as a viable solution. The transition from overindulgence to moderation can be seamless when one continues to participate in pleasurable activities with the act and the desire to be inebriated completely absent.

An unavoidable consequence of an individual who is trying to recover from alcoholism in this culture is association with Alcoholics Anonymous (AA). AA is an organization that supports people who abuse alcohol and wish to quit. With all the good intentions the AA organization has, with all the support for suffering alcoholics, there are practices in AA I will make reference to that I found undesirable and in direct conflict with acquiring a moderate lifestyle. It is not my intention to pass judgment on the individuals who participate in the organization. They are honestly trying to live right and stay sober.

During my association with AA, I was initially disillusioned, and later confused, with the reason an organization with wide spread social acceptance would be able to introduce to its members what is commonly known as negative psychology. For example, "Once and alcoholic, always an alcoholic" is a slogan used in AA that is not in the long term interest of *all* of its members.

I make no claims that I am an authority on alcoholism. I claim only the ability to drink moderately after years of being an alcoholic, and the ability to know why. I have intentionally represented my experiences or views while suggesting alternatives in psychology and behavior as a demonstration or example. I realize the abusive behavior of different individuals will not share the same associated errors in thought or deed; therefore, not all patterns of defeat are mentioned. I have been as thorough as I can, and am confident I will have struck a similar note to the tune of most abusive personalities. Perhaps for some it will be motivation to understand the nature of their perplexing addictive behavior.

Contents

Chapter I

Preliminary

First Misconception

While I was discussing the prospects of this book with interested individuals, it became evident that most people believe that once a person is an alcoholic, he/she will always be an alcoholic. That is, if a person uncontrollably drinks alcohol on a regular basis, he/she will never be able to change and drink moderately on a regular basis without the desire to get drunk. This widespread generalization, though it may well be true for some, is not true for everyone. Some can drink moderately, without the desire to get drunk, after being a full-fledged alcoholic. There are no hidden genes or allergies that dictate behavior, even when a propensity exists.

The "disease" of alcoholism is a combination of psychological conditioning and physical susceptibility. The psychological conditioning can represent a mature avoidance attitude with its associated discontent. There is permission to overindulge. There is the desire to overindulge. There is an association to an enjoyable experience with intoxication. The physical susceptibility to be an alcoholic represents a genetic disposition commonly exacerbated with an inappropriate diet and an overall unhealthy lifestyle.

Psychological conditioning and biological dispositions that can create the propensity to be an alcoholic are *not* immutable influences that possess the individual to act inappropriately. The definable causes of alcoholism have tangible choices in thought and action which can provide the desire not to get drunk.

It is an unfortunate consequence of the prevalent belief, "once an alcoholic, always an alcoholic," that individuals continue to believe they're still alcoholics even though they haven't had a drink in years. If non-practicing alcoholics gave themselves permission to try just one drink, they would go right back to being overindulgent because they *believe* they're alcoholics.

I *was* a practicing alcoholic. Several people respond to my ability to drink moderately with, "You never really were an alcoholic, you just thought you were." I became totally inebriated on a somewhat regular basis for 17 years and now alcoholics, non-practicing alcoholics and individuals who have never been inclined to overindulge indicate I couldn't possibly have been an alcoholic because they all believe an alcoholic could never become a moderate drinker.

Definition of an Alcoholic

The American culture's primary rehabilitation organization, Alcoholics Anonymous, states: "We define an alcoholic as anyone whose drinking disrupts his (or her) business, family or social life and who cannot stop, even though he may want to." Anyone familiar with indulgent behavior will recognize in the above statement, "... cannot stop, even though he may want to" as the most defining aspect of the alcoholic. The worst case of this scenario refers to an individual's ability to drink with complete abandon: when he/she loses track of time, forgets about values, and/or priorities, and drinks one drink after another uncontrollably, as if free will were completely absent and the urge to continue drinking – more and more – has taken on a mind of its own.

Other definitions of alcoholic behavior include: "Heavy alcohol use is defined as drinking five or more drinks per occasion on *five or more days* in the previous 30 days. 'Binge' alcohol use is defined as drinking five or more drinks on the same occasion on at least *one day* in the past 30 days" (Department Of Health And Human Services 87). These definitions are good references, but one does not have to count so many drinks per so many days to know they're an alcoholic. A definition more simply stated is: to drink uncontrollably, to drink in excess, or to wake up with a hangover are all indications of being an alcoholic.

A Word on Semantics

It is a general consensus in literature and in practice that individuals involved with providing counseling avoid using words as have-to, ought, must, imperative, should and never because recipients of that kind of language tend to be defensive, or experience guilt or shame. Avoiding the "all or nothing" imperatives and condescending "oughts," an effective counselor's job is to paint a picture of options that provides *choices*, permitting their clients to experience personal responsibility – a sense of control.

This book uses compulsory language intentionally. From

the perspective of a person who enjoys a sense of well-being, there is a clear distinction between optional and non-optional choices. In reference to moderation being a consistently enjoyable lifestyle, there are very specific "dos" and "don'ts." The suggestion that using the words must, ought, should, or never *should* be avoided leads into a semantic trap, where a restriction in words that connote an imperative is an obvious contradiction in terms, and the real reason certain words are avoided, in the context of discussing non-optional life choices, is because of their effect and not their meaning. It is my intention to communicate adamantly the meaning and the effect of certain aspects of life having absolute value, that are immune to change and are applicable to everyone. It is my hope that in the course of reading this book, it will become evident that moderation is always intrinsically good and a lifestyle of moderation, in which an individual is experiencing a sense of well-being, will include an appropriate diet and exercise (as examples), without exception.

Recovery is a personal choice and I will try to paint a picture of the options; but, the choices are clear and concise, black and white, you either do or you don't. Once the value in moderation is understood and appreciated, there is no ambiguity about which direction your personal choices will take you in reference to whether or not you will participate in alcohol overindulgence. Individuals who experience a sense of well-being are attuned to their core attributes and make choices that are complementary to their physical and mental dispositions, are flexible and open minded, but also have immutable positions on matters like moderation. Under this context, moderation is a *desirable* aspect of life that is a personal choice, not an external directive. Moderation is what *ought* to be and is effortlessly what *must* be done (because they want to), and is what *should never* be deviated from.

This strong language initially sounds harsh or prohibitive, but freedom from alcohol overindulgence is the beginning of a liberating independence. Freedom from alcohol overindulgence represents social and personal freedoms that are absent in individuals who overindulge or who abstain by arguable, restricting thought processes and social contacts – the "all or nothing" alcoholics and non-practicing alcoholics.

The initial definitive language will later be experienced as a mute point to the moderate persons who don't overindulge because they will *enjoy* doing what they *must*, and effortlessly *never* deviate from being what they *ought* because the lifestyle of moderate persons is what they *adamantly want.*

Chapter 2

How I Got to Here from There

The Nightmare

I will tell you briefly how I have come from an alcoholic background in an effort to convince disbelievers that I really was an alcoholic. This is not to be confused with "telling your story," a practice in AA in which members are encouraged to relive their pasts, reiterating their appalling drunk stories, in an effort to convince themselves that they were, and therefore still are, alcoholics.

I started my alcohol abuse in high school as I became rebellious, joined the hippie crowd, and "tuned in and dropped out." My ambition was to stay high and play music on my guitar. At age 24 I married and straightened out enough to get an A.S. degree in electronics, which led to my occupation in electronics, which I still have 20 years later. I was married for six years, during which time I had three children, two sons and a daughter. When my youngest child, my daughter, was one year old and I had been working at my new job for about a year, I was divorced. By then I was a practicing alcoholic.

I remember that driving home from work took a half hour, and I would regularly have two beers finished by the time I got home. I would drink socially; but, when I was overindulgent, I would usually drink by myself. Sometimes I would drink intermittently, perhaps 3 to 4 times per month, but typically in excess – 6 to 12 beers in a 12 hour period. As time progressed, I would get drunk more and more often. The only reason I didn't get drunk at night was because I was either too hungover or felt too guilty from the previous time. My periods of sobriety could last two to three days, but I frequently had to take it to the limit, drink all night, and be completely miserable the next day. For years all my vacation time was taken as a day here and a day there to recover from hangovers.

There were periods of time when I would drink just one six-pack every night, but then I would mess up that routine by drinking two six-packs or more, and not be able to go to work the next day. Primarily I would overindulge with beer, but occasionally I would drink wine or hard-liquor. Sometimes I would mix the different types of alcohol, depending on the occasion. At some time in the middle of my alcoholic career, I became reluctant to drink hard-liquor because of the resulting black-outs. Among other unsavory aspects, black-outs represented the incredibly frightening experience of waking up in the morning and not remembering how or when I made my way into bed.

During the course of my stupors, I would call all my new

and old friends in the middle of the night; I would be so drunk I could hardly talk. I felt the calls were always so important, they couldn't wait. My poor ex-wife was the unfortunate recipient of many middle-of-the-night calls.

I was involved in two trial proceedings as a direct result of my being intoxicated. In one of those proceedings, I was the victim of a stabbing and narrowly escaped death. The doctors told me it was a miracle I was alive – I was stabbed between the two main ventricles of the heart. I was completely drunk. I went right back to drinking three weeks later, as soon as I could. Years after my stabbing incident, there are pictures of me showing how bloated my face was, with signs of liver and kidney damage. I had normally been a thin man; in these pictures I can hardly recognize myself.

I was in and out of AA a couple times, for two years the first time and just less than a year the second time. Take my word for it, I was an alcoholic. One of the things that occurred to me while in AA was that nobody described hangovers like the ones I had. I came close to calling 911 so many times, when I really thought I was dying. It was hard to think I wasn't going to die while experiencing unquenchable dehydration, and with my heart pounding profusely and erratically in my chest.

The Dawning

The conclusion to my overindulgence with alcohol came in the following manner. In order to keep my job, I became a weekend drunk only. I would drink *all night* (no sleep) Friday and *all day* Saturday, then finally crash completely exhausted as I surrendered to sleep (Saturday night). I would be drunk and hungover at the same time, and be completely delirious from sleep deprivation, combined with the effects of not eating anything, except perhaps one meal, over a 24 hour period. Food diminishes the effects of alcohol, and I didn't want to spoil the experience of intoxication. I would finish the weekends by nursing a horrendous hangover all day Sunday, having just a couple maintenance beers and soup when I would try to start eating again. I did this every single weekend for about a year.

Toward the end of this year long period, my parents called me on a Saturday morning, after one of my regular all-night, weekend binges. I was so drunk I couldn't talk. I could not articulate any condolence to my poor mother who was crying at the other end of the phone because her son was so drunk every word he tried to say was with a stammer and an unintelligible, heavy slur.

Although I was completely humiliated and with failing health (I also smoked profusely while I was drinking), I wanted to live. I began to read self-help books, listen to success tapes, meditate, exercise, and study body chemistry and diet – my stomach was always upset. I looked to the strong and wanted their freedom; I *wanted* to be a *moderate person*. I had a strong desire to re-establish my ability to play the guitar and be in bands that played in the local bars. I wanted the pleasure of enjoying a stout while mingling with the crowd. At work I needed a clear head; I needed to develop my skills and make more of a contribution. I wanted my self-esteem back so I could participate in the enjoyment of a normal lifestyle.

Chapter 3

Prerequisites to Moderation

Acknowledgment of Overindulgence

The first prerequisite to rehabilitation, for the practicing alcoholic, is the acknowledgment of overindulgence. It will seem like this point is too obvious to those unfamiliar with alcoholism; but, to those with an exposure to alcoholic behavior, denial will be a very recognizable characteristic. Alcoholics spend years denying they have a problem with alcohol; their whole life can unintentionally become about alcohol, with the suffering and consequences of intoxication overlooked with truly incomprehensible denial. This can represent an individual's inability to accept that he/she is a truly bad or incorrigible person.

It is not uncommon for the overindulgence of alcohol to be intermittent, with periods of abstinence or moderation in-between, as if there is no problem – just sometimes. The developing alcoholic will dodge the acknowledgment of a problem with alcohol by degrees. With comparison to a real alcoholic he/she could say, "I'm not that bad, yet." Another reason denial matures to such proportions can be attributed to the undesirable consequence of rehabilitation – total abstinence. Alcoholics like alcohol and don't want to stop drinking. To them, alcohol is thought of as an integral aspect of feeling good and enjoying life.

If you drink excessive amounts of alcohol, don't deny it; acknowledge your overindulgence and come to terms with your choices. You can continue to suffer the consequences of periodic intoxication; you can stop drinking entirely and practice abstinence; or you can drink moderately. It is my intention that the content of this book will provide the fundamentals to the art of drinking alcohol moderately.

Desire to be Moderate
The next prerequisite to rehabilitation, following the acknowledgment of overindulgence, is to desire to be free of addictive behavior. Any individual contemplating the idea that he/she can be an ex-alcoholic, moderate drinker *has* to have a distinct longing to be free from alcohol overindulgence, and this propensity has to be channeled into a specific goal; that is, the *strong desire to be moderate.* Make the desire to be a moderate individual an attractive and well-defined objective with as many specific details you can think of. Create periodic intervals of time to do this thoroughly.

Maxwell Maltz in *Psycho-Cybernetics* describes the need to have very specific, positive oriented goals. He says, "... the brain and nervous system constitute a marvelous and complex 'goal-striving mechanism,' a sort of built-in automatic guidance system which works *for* you as a 'success mechanism,' or *against* you as a 'failure mechanism' (XIX)." Ex-alcoholic, moderate drinking will not happen by accident. You cannot have a "who cares?" attitude or suffer from apathy. You have to intentionally make it a priority, a desirable objective, a well-defined goal, and then become excited, enthusiastic, including any positive emotion that is applicable – as much as possible.

Don't read any further without getting this point. This is a fundamental concept in acquiring post-alcoholic moderation. An ex-alcoholic will enjoy a moderate lifestyle because he/she *intentionally wants and strongly desires* a moderate lifestyle. This *strong desire* to be moderate will enable an individual to prioritize activities which complement a moderate lifestyle while avoiding activities that don't complement a moderate lifestyle. At first this will be with conscious intention, but later it will become second nature – a fully developed healthy habit pattern. With this desire culminating into appropriate behavior, will come the rewards and sense of well-being that is derived from being moderate.

Openness to Instruction
Another prerequisite to rehabilitation is to be open to instruction. The admission of a problem with alcohol and desire to change can happen by default; but, not being open to instruction can be the primary inhibiting factor to rehabilitation. Being open represents admitting your thought processes aren't quite right and acquiring a willingness to listen to the experts, that is, to individuals whose lives are working. Alcoholics tend to have attitudes that are prohibitive to instruction: "Nobody's gonna tell me what to do," or "I don't want to grow up," or "I just want to have fun." It becomes a duty to be irresponsible and rebellious and act out with alcohol overindulgence.

Even after overcoming my resistance to instruction, my ability to obtain the prerequisites to rehabilitation were not without their difficulties. One of the hardest parts was surrendering to organizations that advocated total abstinence. Abstinence represented a huge conflict of interest. I didn't want to alienate myself from what was considered a normal lifestyle, where alcohol consumption was somewhat common. Also, I enjoyed alcohol and didn't want to be deprived of an occasional drink. I feel very strongly that it was very unfortunate I did not have the option to enter a local rehabilitation program that advocated moderation instead of abstinence.

For the rehabilitating alcoholic, following instruction should not be in conflict with the inner voice or conscience that tells when something is right. Unfortunately, an individual who has a history of abusive behavior will be in the habit of not listening to the inner voice and there will not always be clear options. More amenable options are needed for the individual interested in freedom from alcohol overindulgence. The point is: the rehabilitating alcoholic needs to reconsider his/her previous conditioning and to seek out mentors who model appropriate behavior. Initially, this could feel uncomfortable, but dedication to behavior modification that is in your own best interest is mandatory.

A major point about being open to instruction is that it shouldn't be a concept that's a good idea to try for a period of time; that is, it has to be developed into a consistent attitude of growth and self-improvement. I have the luxury of working around brilliant individuals who absorb information like sponges. For them it's a habit to be always acquiring new applicable information. This requires tremendous concentration, comprehension, and flexibility.

Alcoholics have a tendency to be stuck in time, unconsciously holding onto previous conditioning with an adamant defense that is completely inflexible and narrow-minded. They tend to be on their own self-centered agendas which do not include *positive* self-development. I emphasize "positive" because individuals involved in rehabilitation are not necessarily developing new skills that are in their *best* interest.

For the alcoholic, the absence of development is augmented with the desire to escape and be lazy, with mini vacations exhibited by being high (drunk). It becomes imperative that the individual who suffers from an abusive lifestyle relinquish the escapist, want-to-be-lazy attitude and develop a habit of seeking out information on specific subjects of interest (like moderation) *from individuals who have demonstrated the ability to have life work* in those areas of interest.

Following in the footsteps of an expert represents a shortcut to success. For example, learning how to play tennis will happen easier and faster with appropriate instruction in how to hold the racket, how to follow through, even how to "think" tennis. While considering moderation as an alternative to overindulgence, examine the lives of individuals who drink alcohol moderately and ask why are they able to drink alcohol without the desire to get drunk. Other than that they might not have the genetic propensity, what is their attitude? How are their priorities and values different? How is it that they don't enjoy being drunk like you do? The answers to those questions are addressed in the following chapters.

Acknowledge overindulgence, embrace a strong desire to not get drunk and be open to instruction. Then the arguments and conflicts of interest will subside, as you will no longer *want* to overindulge because you have acquired the thoughts, actions, and identity of a moderate person.

Prerequisites to Moderation, Key Points:

- Acknowledge overindulgence.
- Make the *strong desire* to be moderate an attractive and well-defined objective.
- Be open to instruction.

Chapter 4

The Psychology of Moderation

Eliminating Avoidance Psychology and Discontent

One of the major contributions to my ability to drink moderately was the cessation of specific inappropriate thought. Once I began to identify the *causes* (incorrect thinking) of my alcoholism, I knew I could change the thought, and thereby, change the effects on my circumstances. Thought control is crucial and the content of your mind has everything to do with how you'll act. From the turn of the 19th century, James Allen states, "The aphorism, 'As a man thinketh in his heart so is he,' not only embraces the whole of a man's being, but is so comprehensive as to reach out to every condition and circumstance of his life. A man is literally *what he thinks*, his character being the complete sum of all his thoughts" (2). Other than being gender specific, it captures the essence of how one can participate in a lifestyle of moderation.

For me the most blatant incorrect thought pattern was my

"live for the weekend" mentality. I was an escapist, an avoider, and frequently discontented. I cannot over-emphasize this point. Identifying this escapist thought pattern and understanding *I could choose* not to entertain an avoidance psychology was paramount to my ability to be independent and happy, and changed my life. I had developed the discontentment skills in high school, where every day I said to myself, "I wish I were somewhere else." Mentally, I was hardly present in any of my classes and, consequently, barely passed high school with Cs and Ds in all my academic classes.

Then later on, my rebellious "I don't want to be here" attitude matured to a pathetic drudgery during the work week. Towards the end of my alcoholism, the drudgery of the week would shift to an exhilarating excitement as the hours approached to Friday night, and I knew I was going to get away from it all and get totally blasted (very drunk).

My life changed when I understood and applied the knowledge that once I eliminated present moment incorrect thought patterns, undesirable conditions would subside. These conditions, which I thought were just happening to me, were the direct result of my "wish I were somewhere else" thoughts. Anyone suffering from present moment discontent should never say, "I can't wait for the weekend," "I wish I were somewhere else," or "I can't wait for tomorrow," for tomorrow will never come. Tomorrow you will want tomorrow. The habit of wishing for something different or something perceived as better at a different time grows into *persistent present moment discontent.*

To eliminate the habit of associating the future with being better, it is as simple as observing that whenever you're wanting some future gratification *stop the thought*; don't entertain it. Return to the present moment with any and all of its activities and be in the present, physically and mentally. This is one of the key points in the psychology of moderation. *Insist on the present moment as being the only time to enjoy life.*

Consciously being in the moment can be very difficult if you're giving up substance abuse. It can represent dealing with the feeling of incompleteness – an incredible void, restlessness, dissatisfaction, and need. This is especially true if the present moment is when you would historically be indulging in excessive amounts of alcohol. Acknowledge the incomplete feeling that you're trying to avoid and hang out with it. Don't avoid it. Ask why there's an uncomfortable feeling, other than because of the biological dependence on a drug that your body thinks it wants. Something you ate? Not enough sleep? The kids are screaming? This is the toughest part because you don't feel good; but take heart, it's temporary (more on feeling in Chapter 8).

The live-for-the-weekend attitude, with its avoidance-to-gratification cycle, is always a present moment psychological disposition. This prevalent avoidance psychology will permeate all areas of the addictive personality with compulsive behavior that is not just about alcohol addiction. It is imperative for alcoholics to acknowledge their avoidance psychology, with its cycles of dependence with abusive substances or overindulgence, is not just about alcohol. There are companion drugs that complement or intensify a self-indulgent avoidance mentality. Typically abusive personalities will avoid present moment discontent with cycles of dependence using excessive amounts of alcohol, coffee, sugar or unhealthy substances, like cigarettes, exotic drugs or narcotics.

Cycles of dependence on multiple substances are an identifying marker of individuals suffering from discontent. People suffering from alcoholism will nurse their avoidance psychology with an assortment of substances throughout the day and use unhealthy substances and/or overindulgence as a fix (like drugs) to appease their compulsive behavior. Indulgent individuals will frequently have in the back of their minds that they are able to endure the present moment because later at break-time with a cigarette, or tonight with a six-pack (as examples), they can reward themselves. They can fix their mood or disposition with some abusive, indulgent, compulsive habit that feeds and maintains their avoidance-to-gratification cycle.

All you have is the present moment, even if you're avoiding it by wishing you were somewhere else or feeling something different. Even when you're close to some gratifying event never say, "Now I can relax," because you have a drink or some other fix. It becomes a psychological predisposition to always want a drink or some other substance, in order to feel good at some other time. The problem is in inappropriately trying to satisfy the basic need to feel good.

It also disproportionately distributes feeling good or feeling better in blocks of time. That means in order to feel good or better, you'll cycle to the next drink, or perhaps cigarette, and the time in between will be spent in anticipation of the next drink or cigarette. The tendency is not to appreciate the present moment unless you're using some drug.

STOP anticipating the future as being better as a result of an escapist compulsive habit. Right now is all one has and it's not about using some drug in order to feel good. Anticipate present moment contentment and satisfaction to the best of your ability. Embrace the present. Healthy individuals are not resisting their present moments with an investment in some future event to make them happy. The enjoyable cycles of a healthy lifestyle do not involve fixes for discontentment by using unhealthy substances and/or overindulgence.

The argument for not anticipating the future as being better is: "I need to plan for the future to make things better." I'm not talking about planning for the future, I'm talking about resisting the present; that is present moment discontent. It's healthy to anticipate and plan for good things; furthermore, it is appropriate to work through unfortunate circumstances, in the present, if some kind of discomfort presents itself. The problem with alcoholics is that they're infrequently satisfied with the present; the resisting, avoiding, or craving exemplifies their lives. Even when alcoholics are drunk, they bounce from euphoria to discontent or persistent need. It's always the next drink that will make them happy, and the next drink, and the next drink; and, that's one reason they can't stop drinking.

Again, one of the challenges of the rehabilitating individual is to acknowledge and come to terms with present moment discontent. Happiness is a present moment conscious decision – an attitude – that comes from the inside, not something from out there at some other time. If you depend on drugs to make yourself happy, then you are a slave to them, and cycle in-between "highs" with present moment discontent.

Everyone is dependent on a healthy lifestyle in order to feel good, with good food, healthy habits, satisfying relationships, a sense of purpose, and a safe environment being some of the attributes that make it possible. If you compensate for the absence of a healthy lifestyle with alcohol, you interfere with your natural ability to feel good in the present, with a cycle of dependence on a drug. Eliminating an avoidance psychology with its associated discontent is crucial to independence from alcohol and to acquiring the ability to drink moderately.

Associating Pleasure with Harmful-Habit Patterns

On the issue of associating pleasure with harmful habit patterns, it is imperative to understand that it is *because* a person associates pleasure with harmful habit patterns that he/she is able to perform harmful habit patterns. Anthony Robbins in his *Personal Power Program For Unlimited Success* communicates quite effectively, "Everything we do in life comes from our need to avoid pain and our desire to gain pleasure." One of the perplexing and contradictory aspects of an abusive personality is its ability to endure so much mental anguish and physical pain. How can that be if what we do comes from our need to avoid pain and our desire to gain pleasure?

It can be argued by the alcoholic, "All those hangovers never kept me from the next drink." Conversely, several times I woke up with a hangover and said to myself, "I can't believe it; this is it, I quit (drinking)." The desire to quit drinking in the initial stages of a hangover, with subsequent inability to remain sober, is one of the common, perplexing characteristics of alcoholics in general. The problem in thinking the pain of a hangover will actually keep alcoholics from overindulging again, though it can be motivating, is that they immediately go forward in an effort to feel better. How do they feel better? By getting drunk again. It's not necessarily on a conscious level of thinking; their bodies know intoxication is associated with huge amounts of endorphins.

Endorphins are amino acids that react with opiate receptor sites in the brain; they create a sense of well-being by minimizing physical and psychological pain. While making reference to the effects of alcohol by its relationship to the opiate receptor sites in the brain, Dr. Kathleen DesMaisons, an addictive nutrition specialist states, "It does not act on the receptor directly, as narcotics do, but causes the brain to release additional beta-endorphin to produce the high we associate with drinking" (68-69).

You can be motivated to stop uncontrollable drinking by the pain of a hangover, but it is the physiological and psychological association of pleasure in being drunk that keeps you addicted. The endorphin levels are combined with the enjoyment of rituals around being drunk, including the anticipation and planning for the next opportunity to feel really good (get drunk) between drunks.

The solution to this dilemma is not to associate being drunk as pleasurable. This is easier than you think. Just list all the things about being intoxicated that are undesirable. Don't just think about items on a list, grab a pencil and paper and write them down. If you do this honestly, this list will completely outweigh any benefits you've identified with being inebriated. Feed this list to your brain every day, add to it, make it a constant companion, for it is one of the *keys* to independence from alcohol addiction.

The exercise of not associating intoxication with pleasure is not an option. Don't leave room for, "Just once in a while is OK," or "I really want to, but sometimes it just doesn't work out." Totally, without reservation, smash any association with being drunk as pleasurable, not just the easy stuff like the hangover, but being "high," also. Acknowledge being high as the enemy, where a subjective exaggerated state of euphoria, with intense sensitivity, *masks* the despicable, needy, unstable, dependent, disgusting, obnoxious, embarrassing, indulgent, non-cognizant. Remove the mask that separates subjective inebriation from objective reality and you will never want to get drunk again. Especially remove any association of being high as being pleasurable by simultaneously experiencing all the undesirable aspects.

When the subjective high is relegated to a minuscule nothing by being overshadowed – completely outweighted – by its undesirable companions, inebriation is out of the question. Don't read any further without getting this point. This *alone* will keep an individual from overindulging. This is one of the key thought processes of moderation. This is the psychology of moderation. This is the foundation, the cornerstone that all else can be built on: Moderate individuals do not want to get drunk because they *view intoxication as undesirable.*

Thoroughly list all the undesirable aspects of intoxication and emotionally loathe the prospect of being drunk. The concept of not associating feeling good with feeling high came to me as an enlightening experience and it enabled me to drink moderately. It came as a feeling, and I *knew* I no longer wanted to overindulge.

If feeling good by being uninhibited and carefree is frequently the result of being under the influence of alcohol, ask yourself, "How uninhibited and carefree is alcohol addiction?" The concept that one cannot associate intoxication with being a pleasurable experience is perhaps one of the hardest to grasp; it involves a definite shift in perspective. It's like suggesting that if I were to remember back when I was drunk, I wasn't high, feeling good or having fun. Or when a good joke teller is able to make the audience laugh hysterically from the silly escapades of a drunk story, we don't have to wonder why it's funny. We don't need to psychoanalyze why reminiscing our suffering or being the fool can sometimes be humorous. Finding humor in a drunk story is not indicative of wanting to be drunk.

Select all of the times you were inebriated and try playing them back as if they were recorded on video tape, and now your friends and family are watching them with you. Are you proud of them? Still feeling good? Still having fun? Most people would experience embarrassment and shame. If you find humor in some of it, it doesn't matter. The only thing that matters is that any individual wanting to be moderate will find him/herself independent from the desire to get drunk by viewing the subjective high from alcohol overindulgence with extreme distaste.

Again, realize the reason moderate individuals don't ever get drunk is because they *don't want to get drunk*. Moderate individuals don't believe getting drunk is a good or pleasurable thing to do and are never tempted to think otherwise. Understand what not *wanting* to get drunk implies unquestionably detesting the possibility, being repelled by it, finding being drunk disgusting and repulsive. If you don't *want* to get drunk, you won't.

There are some who could say, "But I don't want to get drunk, it just happens. I actually wish I could stop sometimes, but I just can't." Try to understand that one of the fundamental reasons why a person overindulges, even if there's conflict, or even if it's not on a conscious level, is the desire or pleasure from being intoxicated. Put that desire under a microscope in your mind and internally come to grips with intoxication or being high not being synonymous with feeling good.

Also, understand not wanting to overindulge is not an exercise in "willpower." This implies an individual's ability to *discipline* his/her actions by staying sober, even though he/she may *want* to drink excessive amounts of alcohol. The volition to stay sober comes from the *honest desire to be clear headed and sober.* For the moderate individual, avoiding intoxication is not a forced discipline; it is an effortless commitment to a desirable self-image.

Review your list of the undesirable aspects of being intoxicated and add to it. Be thorough. To enjoy life is to be free from alcohol addiction, to have rewarding relationships and the sense of well-being associated with a moderate lifestyle. It is important to remove any and all associations with being drunk as pleasurable.

Associating Pleasure with Moderation

In order to be successful, the goal to acquire a *strong desire* to be moderate (one of the prerequisites to moderation), *has* to be augmented with positive feelings. That is, *associate pleasure with moderation.* For me this concept really shut the door on my abusive behavior. This is the next step and the companion to believing that being drunk is undesirable. Experience moderation as the most rewarding and satisfying feeling. Create a list of all the reasons why you would feel great if you had control over alcohol. Make sure your list of the desirable aspects of moderation is written on paper. Don't just think about it.

As you're creating your list, visualize enjoying one drink and only one drink. Feel the pleasure in having a new sense of control. Acknowledge all the freedom this represents.

Experience the pleasure of being in control. Make your whole life about the pleasure of moderation. You are the personification of a moderate person. Make it your religion. Worship moderation. Adhere to it so intimately that you could never act in a manner that would be inconsistent with it. Some might say this is getting a little carried away, but I could not be more adamant: you have to be, eat, sleep, drink 110% moderation.

I realize this could sound like some kind of fanaticism, but being a moderate person is the natural way to be; it is the natural way to feel. If the return to normal – natural – moderation feels or sounds like unwarranted devoutness, it is only because it addresses the return from the extreme mental distortions and behavior of an alcoholic. Remember, I'm addressing the addictive personality; if temptations come, you lose. Don't make it a contest of the will; you will fail.

Again, it is not a contest of the will; you are not tempted because it is against your very nature. You are the embodiment of moderation, unquestionably and always. It is your identity: "I am a moderate person." Because you *believe* you are a moderate person, appreciate and understand what it means, and because it represents a pleasurable experience, you *never want* to act in a manner that is inconsistent with how you feel; you are never tempted.

Don't read any further without getting this point. This is another key concept in the psychology of moderation. One *has* to associate a pleasurable experience with moderation. This is a major point: How you *feel* and what you believe yourself to be have everything to do with how you'll act. Every thought should complement the identity of being a moderate person as an enjoyable experience. Psychologically scale the subjective high from intoxication so that it pales in comparison to the "big picture" of moderation. Make the difference in this comparison HUGE. Use the list of pleasurable aspects of moderation as an aid in scaling a moderate lifestyle as *much more* significant, and *much more* rewarding, than periodic intoxication. Be incredibly thorough with your list of the pleasurable aspects of moderation and you will not only want to be moderate, but, you will lose the desire to be overindulgent.

When considering the pleasurable aspects of moderate alcohol consumption you could include the health benefits. There is scientific evidence that moderate alcohol consumption can be good for the health of some, aiding in digestion and enhancing the blood's circulation. Also, there is evidence that individuals who enjoy moderate alcohol consumption, statistically, have healthier moderate lifestyles with better diets than those who abstain or who are overindulgent (Raloff 53).

The relaxing aspects of drinking in moderation can add to enjoyable social contacts. One of the most frequently stated complaints I've heard, and have personally experienced, was the discomfort felt by abstinent or overindulgent individuals during social gatherings where alcohol is served. Experiencing discomfort is not true for everyone and there are varying degrees of unpleasantness, but in general, the abstinent feel out-of-place and conspicuous, perhaps envious of those who can control their drinking. The overindulgent, if not too far gone, will attempt to act responsibly and pace themselves in an effort to not act the fool, depending on their mood.

If it is your intention to be an ex-alcoholic moderate drinker, acknowledge your option to drink responsibly during social gatherings, as opposed to being abstinent or overindulgent, as the most enjoyable, satisfying and rewarding experience. LIST everything you can think of that establishes moderation as an attractive, desirable experience over the alternative options of abstinence or overindulgence, and you will acquire the effortless will to be moderate.

Once an individual *feels* like he/she is a moderate person, that enjoyable experience will permeate all aspects of his/her life, including the way a he/she acts, so that the doing (not overindulging) is effortless and feels natural. Moderate people do not have to remind themselves to drink moderately or be disciplined about alcohol consumption; they effortlessly don't overindulge because they don't *want* to overindulge.

Separating From Adversity
One of the consequences of being an alcoholic is low self-esteem. Years of hangovers program the mind with early morning affirmations from, "I am an idiot," to using an assortment of curse words combined with overwhelming remorse and shame. It could take years to establish a sense of self-worth while trying to eliminate inappropriate habit patterns and negative psychology. One of the easiest ways to recover is to *think or say only that which is in your best interest.* Always observe your mental and verbal dialogue and ask if the content of what you think or say is what you really want in your life. As a recovering alcoholic, you may find it hard to be in the present enough to observe this, or even be clear-headed enough to know what you want, but always remember: think or say that which is in your best interest to the best of your ability. Religiously separate yourself from adversity in thought and word.

This is augmenting the observation of your thought patterns previously mentioned, as living for the weekend thoughts, while observing your speech. Pay attention to everything you say. Your speech will be most revealing. Catch yourself when saying anything that sounds like dissatisfaction, discontent or victim language and stop it. Don't think it and don't say it. The world will keep on turning without your complaining.

The problem with the alcoholic mind is that it is justified in discontent. Alcoholics feel justified or entitled to a good drunk – they deserve it. The rational defense for discontent is: "I wouldn't be realistic if I didn't complain about this." The point is this: It is your justified defense and discontent that keeps you in unpleasant circumstances. It's a loop. The only way to escape is to stop complaining (force yourself at first) and to accept the situation, while acknowledging choices that are in your best interest. Replace discontentment with acceptance and present moment satisfaction to the best of your ability. Then, by your focusing on what is in your best interest, what is best will come into your life.

As you pursue what you want, seek out applicable mentors and models in behavior and psychology and follow them. There are many books, tapes and seminars on how to succeed. Find the ones that are applicable to your needs and use them. Constantly feed your mind information and ideas that complement a lifestyle of moderation.

Strive to be the *best* at what you do and constantly look for opportunities to grow and enjoy life. Emulate your ideal self. Always think and say what's in your best interest, and it will come into your life. Don't ever get drunk. You should honestly know it is *never* appropriate. Moderation is the key.

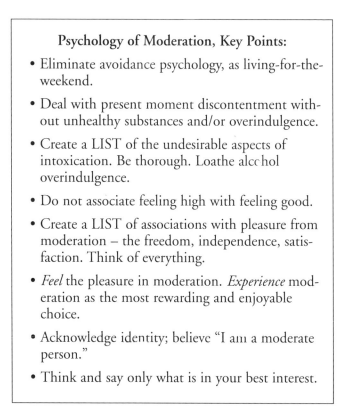

Psychology of Moderation, Key Points:

- Eliminate avoidance psychology, as living-for-the-weekend.

- Deal with present moment discontentment without unhealthy substances and/or overindulgence.

- Create a LIST of the undesirable aspects of intoxication. Be thorough. Loathe alcohol overindulgence.

- Do not associate feeling high with feeling good.

- Create a LIST of associations with pleasure from moderation – the freedom, independence, satisfaction. Think of everything.

- *Feel* the pleasure in moderation. *Experience* moderation as the most rewarding and enjoyable choice.

- Acknowledge identity; believe "I am a moderate person."

- Think and say only what is in your best interest.

Chapter 5

The Lifestyle of Moderation

Values

Lifestyle is defined as the way a person chooses to live. It indicates the preferences of the individual's priorities, values. This brings up the displacement of values in the alcoholic's mind. Anytime people's values lead them to be self-indulgent and self-destructive, they have a huge conflict of interest. It is imperative that those with a history of being indulgent acknowledge their values. Honestly list everything that is of value to you. I suggest sobriety and peace of mind be at the top, but list everything.

It is important not to judge, just to list – even including being "high." Notice the conflict in the list; you might have valued being periodically high and healthy on the same list. Acknowledge that conflict of interest. Then create a second list of values that has no conflict by including only positive attributes, as health, companionship, moderation, and all of the things that are most important to you. Post it. Internalize it. Your list of values will expose that being drunk is not in your best interest.

Your values will point you to what you want in life and vice-versa. For example, "I want pot roast and a beer" could represent that you value home-cooking and moderation with alcohol. This might seem frivolous, but realize that a lot of people don't know what they want and what they value. How cognizant of amenable values is the alcoholic while bouncing from hangover to intoxication? The more you know what you want and what you value, the more you will find those qualities present in your life. On the other hand, if you don't know what your values are, or what you want out of life, you will never find them in your life accidentally.

Be aware that acknowledging what you value doesn't mean those ideals will inevitability appear in your life. If there is conflict with what you value and what you experience, then you can realize that we are all subject to our primary conditioning. We have bits and pieces of information that we choose to believe, with no guarantee that we have acquired the most appropriate instruction for our lives.

That is, even if you have a suitable value in some aspect in your life, it doesn't mean you have the adequate instruction to incorporate it successfully. Take full responsibility for aspects of your life that you value, and in the areas that aren't working seek guidance. Again, this means being open to instruction. Clearly define what's important in your life by acknowledging your values. Be completely committed to working on areas that aren't satisfactory and eliminate conflicts of interest.

Freedom – not License

When I graduated from high school, I felt my diploma represented a license to freedom, a license to embrace anarchy, with no thoughts of values, integrity, rules, or remorse. Years later, after suffering the consequences of my ill-fated, inappropriate choices, it became apparent to me that the only freedom a person has is to be what he/she ought. This means being engaged in activities as a result of personal choices representing the *acceptance* (favorable reception) of appropriate responsibilities. In the event a person is not able to do what he/she ought, whether self-imposed or otherwise, there is an absence of freedom.

For those who have a history of chronic alcoholism, having a clear sense of their ultimate destiny, what they ought to be doing, could be difficult to ascertain. Even an aptitude test (which should be administered to all individuals entering institutional rehabilitation) can only serve as a guide, and may not necessarily coincide with a person's area of significant contribution. It could be a distressing situation when adhering to guidance on how to make a contribution is incompatible with listening to the dictates of the heart.

To make matters worse, the confusion in trying to understand how to appropriately participate comes during a period of time when the behavior modification of no longer being self-indulgent will also be unavoidably uncomfortable. The key is to maintain sobriety and listen to the dictates of the heart. It is appropriate activity done with passion that is done best.

People who know what they ought to be doing are closely linked to the acknowledgment of their values, with an emphasis on appropriate behavior. There is a synergy of values and behavior, suitable values combined with doing what ought to be done, that is realized as being as free as one can get. There is no such thing as freedom when it is in disregard of your own best interest and well-being, or in the demise of someone else. No one could never comprehend the experience of freedom while being a slave to alcohol. Even though some might think they have the right or freedom to get drunk, they will *experience* freedom only by aligning with their ideal selves.

The desire for freedom is a prerequisite to independence from alcohol and acquiring the ability to drink moderately. *Ultimate* freedom is the ability of people to do what they feel they ought. In the event that people are about the business of doing what they ought to be doing, even though invariably this represents hard work, they have a sense of purpose. It represents commitment to responsibilities with the feeling that the individual is in the right place, at the right time, doing the right thing.

This is in contrast to the previously mentioned attitude of the alcoholic: resisting responsibilities, experiencing discontent, and wishing to be somewhere else. Addressing the issue of self-fulfillment as a consequence of complete engagement, Mihaly Csikszentmihalyi in *Finding Flow* says ".. it is to be happy while doing things that stretch our skills, that help us grow and fulfill our potential" (122).

As an ex-alcoholic your lifestyle will change with the acknowledgment of appropriate values; with an appreciation of what you ought to be doing, you will find the absence of discontent. Acquire a lifestyle in which preferences in behavior and activities are always in your best interest, and in the best interest of others.

Associations

Another important aspect of a person's lifestyle is the association with other individuals for whom there is considerable regard. This is the group that one models oneself after. Brian Tracy in *The Luck Factor*, while making reference to Dr. David McClelland's research at Harvard University states, "The members of your reference group will have more of an impact on your success and happiness than any other choices you make in life." Because rehabilitating alcoholics usually have long-time drinking companions, they may find that fact represents the toughest part of their ability to stay sober.

A shift in who you chose to befriend is not trivial. Some people need companionship more than others, and acquiring a new set of social contacts before eliminating the old is not an overnight event. Don't let the difficulty undermine the objective of removing close associations with individuals who drink excessively. This is not an option. Separation from drinking companions and persons with abusive behavior is essential.

You also have to seek out, befriend, and identify with the individuals with the most integrity. In the interim you may find yourself alone more often than you care to be, but that doesn't have to be such a terrible time. It might feel bad at first, but realize that the happiest individuals are too busy being involved with the business of being what they ought rather than worried about being alone. Also realize that birds of a feather do flock together. By being a person of integrity and by having a sense of well-being, you will attract friends with integrity and a sense of well-being.

If the individuals you identify with are those who claim, "I am an alcoholic," then on the basis of that negative psychology (using negative affirmations), you might want to reconsider their companionship.

Control

One of the responsibilities of the moderate individual is to acknowledge control. Control is everything. Brian Tracy in his *Psychology of Achievement* emphatically makes the point: "The level of a person's ability to experience a sense of well-being is proportional to the amount of control they think they have." During the years of my formal education I can't remember ever being specifically counseled to be in control. I received instruction on how to do things, but the specifics never translated to an appreciation for the significance of control, in general. By default I learned that a sense of well-being was experienced by being high on drugs or alcohol and that escaping my responsibilities was fun. Being out of control through inebriation was subjectively acceptable behavior. I never associated feeling good with being in control and not being indulgent. It wasn't until I acknowledged control itself as an experience that superimposes all activity that I was able to appreciate its significance.

Individuals with a propensity to be alcoholic should acknowledge the attributes of being in control. Acknowledging what one has control over can lead to an understanding of how control is different from acceptance or how control complements acceptance. With an appreciation for control a person can recognize that accepting responsibility is how control starts, and enhances the prosperous, fully functioning individual. The ex-alcoholic needs to abhor being out of control to the point that he/she does not have permission to entertain intoxication as an enjoyable option.

Alcoholics, those with abusive personalities, lack control.

Alcoholics don't perceive or acknowledge (because of their denial) that lack of control is an issue. Ex-alcoholics should consider how much control they have over all issues: attitude, thoughts, emotions, health, finances, what to eat, how much to eat, how much sleep to get, what to drink, how much to drink, whom to befriend, and how to react to circumstances outside of their sphere of control. The greater the number of issues they feel they have control over, the better they'll feel.

Individuals who become inebriated on a regular basis are in the habit of being out of control and associate being out of control with being wild, and uninhibited, doing something that's fun and exciting. The rehabilitated individual will replace the excitement and fun of uncontrolled intoxication with the pleasure of a moderate lifestyle. The contentment experienced with being in control will be completely satisfying and so the desire to be inebriated or out of control will be totally absent.

On the issue of control and alcohol, you either have it or you don't. If you don't have the control to be moderate, then don't drink. Control over alcohol is not a concept, it is a knowing. There is a clear, discernible feeling with no ambiguity or doubt. You either know beyond the shadow-of-a-doubt that you don't want to get drunk, or you don't. If you don't know that you don't want to get drunk, then don't drink.

Ex-alcoholic, moderate drinkers cannot take moderation for granted. They can never be careless, lose track of time or get "caught in the moment." They don't find themselves drinking too much because it just snuck up on them. Someone might say, "Gee, that doesn't sound like very much fun." Words like "fun" in reference to alcohol overindulgence and just letting it all hang out are not in the vocabulary of an ex-alcoholic, moderate drinker.

The desire to be uninhibited and carefree is natural, but it is not indicative of being intoxicated or out of control. Contrarily, the more control a person has, the more carefree and free of restraint they will feel. It is the absence of feeling carefree that contributes to the propensity to be a substance abuser, to desire alcohol or other substances to feel uninhibited.

People who use alcohol to have fun or just get loose are displaying a clear indication they are not OK with themselves. There is a need to escape by altering how they feel. People who want to have fun using alcohol must realize the issue is not about having fun. It's all about escaping, avoiding, or masking the fact that they can't have fun or enjoy life without alcohol.

Remember, moderate drinkers do not *want* to get drunk. They are not attracted to intoxication as if it were desirable, pleasurable, or "fun." It is quite satisfying to sip one drink for a long time, and have the presence of mind not to get carried away. You not only feel good about being moderate, you feel great that outside influences cannot compromise your integrity. And you never have a hangover.

Lifestyle of Moderation, Key Points:

- Create a list of values that contains no conflicts of interest.

- Know what you want and what you value.

- Be about the business of being who you ought to be.

- Acquire new social contacts. Have only positive, successful persons as reference companions.

- Understand that a sense of well-being is proportional to the amount of control a person has.

- Don't drink at all if you don't have the control to be moderate.

Chapter 6

Applicable Attitudes

Appreciation

How can an individual who is overindulgent with alcohol fully comprehend the subtleties of existence and have an appreciation for life? Not very easily. He/she will experience intense, exaggerated states of euphoria and mind-boggling hangovers that result in states of depression. A prevalent attitude of gratitude and persistent sense of well-being will elude the overindulgent.

Ex-alcoholic, moderate drinkers must acknowledge an appreciation for life. It is an exercise in not having an avoidance psychology. That is, appreciation for life exercised by moderation is the opposite behavior of the avoidance and discontent experienced by the overindulgent. This sense of appreciation can be subtle and reach into all areas of an individual's life; therefore, nothing is exempt from the consideration of some level of appreciation. Typically, the alcoholic is in the habit of experiencing discontent. It is the ex-alcoholic's responsibility to develop the habit of experiencing an appreciation for as much as possible.

Contentment belongs to the thankful. To be grateful for one's lot in life is to experience joy. A prevalent attitude of gratitude is to anticipate the best and not lament, not regret, but appreciate the past for its lessons in whatever guises the hand of fate may have dealt. Being thankful is being grateful for the past and appreciating the opportunities available in the future; furthermore, it represents a more subtle, present moment, underlying attitude that will prohibit the desire to alter one's experience by ingesting exorbitant amounts of alcohol.

Independence

After alcoholics admit they are powerless over alcohol, are no longer in denial, and wish to be free of alcohol addiction, there is a high probability that they will submit to a rehabilitation organization. Others may unintentionally find themselves in a rehabilitation organization as a consequence of an alcohol related offense; that is, any alcohol related offense in a court of law will typically incur a mandatory sentence of so many AA meetings. The need for rehabilitation organizations that provide a supportive environment for abstinence and guidance is apparent; but, unfortunately these programs, intended for behavioral modification, use what is commonly known as negative psychology as part of their regimen. Going beyond the need to address the denial stages, where alcoholics deny they have drinking problems, these organizations reinforce the belief that members will always be dependent on alcohol and on membership indefinitely by requiring members to reiterate the mandatory motto, "I am an alcoholic."

This debilitating statement should be replaced with positive affirmations as, "I choose sobriety," or, "I am a moderate person." Rehabilitation organizations that have the absence of positive psychology training create the expectation that the members will fail unless they adhere to membership indefinitely, with "once an alcoholic, always an alcoholic" as one of their mottoes. The focus on "defects of character" and "moral inventory" do not instruct applicable behavior modification that utilizes positive psychology.

Typically, individuals seeking solace from alcoholism are like sponges, open to instruction. What they need is encouragement to be the best at what they're good at, and surveys or instructional programs to accumulate information on options if they don't know what they're good at. With the intention of empowering individuals with independence and freedom from the desire to be indulgent, proactive rehabilitation organizations would be of immense service if they were to provide mandatory classes on nutrition and exercise, and stress control classes. Members would be required to know the specifics of the model of a healthy person and memorize them, with a commitment to emulate a healthy person. This could include a specific code of ethics with a commitment to integrity.

It would be highly beneficial to have exercises that would enable members to realize that being drunk is not in their best interest; that feeling good is not synonymous with being high; that being rebellious or having an avoidance psychology is not in their best interest. The expectation should be that the rehabilitating individual will become independent, not only from mentoring programs or the court system, but independent of the desire to drink excessive amounts of alcohol. Indefinite membership in a society for sobriety, or a society for abstinence, could be commendable, but these societies should never set the expectation that members will *never* be able to be independent of membership or alcohol overindulgence, as they do now.

An alcoholic coming from a supposedly "self-centered" agenda to a rehabilitation organization (according to AA, alcoholics are self-centered), where the search for meaning in life or the sense of well-being is exhibited as a warm feeling by praying to God with a group of people, should not preclude programs that teach the psychological tools to enable recipients to enjoy life independently. Every effort should complement the objective: to enable individuals to independently feel free from the desire to alter their body chemistry with drugs in order to feel good.

Once again, alcoholics or occasional drunks who are no longer in denial, admit to needing help, and are open to instruction should adhere to empowering models that provide the concrete examples in psychology and behavior. They should be thoroughly supported and tended to like newborn babes; and as with newborn babes, the objective should be to create fully functioning, independent, self-reliant individuals, not only free from the destructive behavior, but also from the inappropriate thought patterns that culminate in abusive lifestyles.

Confidence

During the rehabilitation process, when recovering alcoholics look around to access the damage, they may notice one of the most valuable characteristics that appears to be missing in themselves is confidence. One of the attributes of successful people (those who acquire favorable results) is their ability to act with confidence, purpose and intent. Confidence is not just an attitude; it is the display or demonstration of courage and faith. Consistent, repeatable, appropriate behavior, attributes of the moderate individual, will complement confidence and vice versa. People who are successful at what they do always have a clear, definable objective and use the same approach or process to problem solving.

One of the steps in the success process is to act with confidence that the solutions already exist. Another step is to be totally committed to each endeavor. Also, failure is not to be viewed as "failure," but rather as an opportunity to learn or to be viewed as a developing experience. Therefore, one will try again and persist. The objective is a definable prospect and the process (confidence, total commitment and persistence) has the absence of restraint. As with a child learning to ride a bicycle, there is the clear objective to ride the bike. They intuitively know they will succeed (confidence) and they're totally committed and persist. This child-like behavior is carried over into adulthood, but can easily become lost when a person participates in the abusive behavior of an alcoholic.

I recall that during the height of my alcoholic period I lacked confidence that the solutions to my problems already existed. I was half-hearted in action and lacked commitment. Failure was always a humiliating experience, not a learning experience.

Occasional drunks will rationalize their behavior by complimenting themselves on how well they juggle between their hangovers and their responsibilities. It's the "getting away with it" denial stage. The feeling of being good at getting away with intoxication and the resulting hangovers creates the illusion of control or confidence. This is a denial not only of the abusive behavior, but also of the causes, which are destructive, negative thought patterns and discontent.

Mature alcoholics lack the courage to try new or challenging endeavors – to go where they have not gone before. Alcoholics tend to find their confidence in a bottle. The abusive lifestyle of a practicing alcoholic destroys self-esteem. At the end of my abusive lifestyle, deep down inside, I thought of myself as the most despicable creature on the face of the earth.

The prerequisite to having confidence is having high self-esteem and unconditional self-acceptance. This prerequisite of self-acceptance is hard to come by after living with alcoholism, but with persistent determination and consistent, repeatable, appropriate behavior, exhibited in having a moderate lifestyle, you can develop it. I noticed that the pace of my return to confidence coincided with how I felt. The conditioned responses that resulted in feelings of shame, remorse, and low self-esteem, combined with the biochemical adjustments from the ravages of alcoholism, prevented me from having a sense of well-being and confidence.

Have clear definable objectives and goals, and develop skills in those areas of interest, and be the *best* you can be. Have the expectation that the solutions to problems already exist, be thoroughly committed, and persist. Acknowledge the model of confidence and emulate it. It is a characteristic easily lost in the self-abusive personality.

Avoiding Powerlessness
One of the prevalent psychological characteristics of alcoholics is powerlessness. Alcoholics aren't just powerless over alcohol, they have an "I give up," surrendering attitude that permeates several aspects of their lives. When alcoholics enter rehabilitation groups, they are introduced to the 12-Steps of

AA from *Twelve Steps and Twelve Traditions.* The very first Step is to admit they are powerless over alcohol. AA wants alcoholics to admit they're powerless over alcohol as a way to demonstrate they are no longer in denial. However, admitting to uncontrollably drinking alcohol, and agreeing to abstinence in order to put the pieces of their lives back together should never infer that those participating in rehabilitation will *never* know why they overindulged, or that they will be powerless *indefinitely* over alcohol.

An individual who reiterates "I am powerless" is affirming, through negative affirmation, that he/she is an individual who will always be powerless. If an individual chooses to adhere to abstinence, that person could replace "powerless over alcohol" with something, as "I have the *power to not drink*," or "*I choose sobriety.*" These are empowering statements that take the recovering individual beyond the denial stages of the practicing alcoholic.

Powerlessness is a psychological disposition that should be shunned. Avoid an attitude where you just want to skate through life and get away with doing as little as possible. Reject a desire to be lazy and stay high, and never give yourself permission not to be developing mentally, physically and spiritually.

Applicable Attitudes, Key Points:

- Appreciation for multiple facets of life will prohibit the desire to get drunk

- Independence is being self-reliant, free of destructive behavior and inappropriate thought patterns.

- Confidence is acting with purpose and intent, courage and faith.

- The success process involves defining a goal and performing the objectives with confidence, total commitment and persistence.

- Powerlessness should be shunned. Repeat with feeling empowering statements as, "I choose sobriety."

Chapter 7

The Action of Moderation

Diet

What we consume as food and drink for subsistence can never be viewed as trivial, especially by substance abuse individuals. To enable my body to recover from the ravages of alcohol abuse, I spent a significant amount of time reading books on nutrition and trying different diets.

Authoritative sources with information about diet and nutrition can be controversial and contradictory. There's debate about how much fat and what kind of fats are best; how much protein or which sources of protein should be consumed. Appropriate sources of carbohydrates and the percent of intake is very controversial. The issues of what affects our mood is separated from blood sugar levels to brain chemistry. Some sources state that blood sugar levels can influence a person's mood, other sources argue a person's mood is primarily the result of brain chemistry, independent of blood sugar levels.

Even with a certain amount of debate, a consensus on

what constitutes a healthy diet can still be gleamed. With trial and error, one can determine an appropriate diet. Alcoholics frequently have imbalances in their diets and exacerbate the problem by over drinking. One consensus from all sources is that *only moderate to no alcohol* consumption is acceptable for a healthy disposition.

With diet and body chemistry being truly unique for different people, the volume of consumption of different types of foods varies; but for optimum health, the ratio of eating from the food groups *tends* to be the same. Everyone needs to find his/her own balance in carbohydrates, protein, fats, vitamins, and minerals. The key is balance. Each person needs to listen to his/her own body. Some individuals tolerate more carbohydrates than others; some individuals, like myself, need significant servings of protein regularly throughout the day.

Maintaining a healthy diet enables an individual to avoid the feeling of being tired and vulnerable. We are biochemical machines and all food and drink is an influencing chemical and should be viewed as such. Eating is not just an exercise in satisfying the palate; it changes our biochemical balance and our physical and mental dispositions. For a rehabilitating alcoholic, the pursuit of acquiring optimum health through diet is not an option. Optimum health has to be one of the items on your list of values.

Though what we eat is an integral aspect of our well-being, the common American diet can be marginal in value by lacking substantial nutrients and containing concentrated carbohydrates. It took me longer than I care to admit to figure out that I was hypersensitive to sugar. American foods are permeated with sweeteners. There are very few processed foods that don't have some form of sugar, labeled as glucose, sucrose, fructose, lactose, or dextrose. Individuals with a sugar sensitive disposition have more opiate receptors in the brain and have an exaggerated response to sugar and alcohol. Dr. Kathleen DesMaisons, in her book about sugar sensitivity, *Potatoes not Prozac* states, "… sugar-sensitive people respond to the bata-endorphin effect of sugar in a bigger way because they naturally have so many more receptors. For them, eating sugar can be like drinking alcohol! Sugar can make us funny, relaxed, silly, talkative and temporarily self-confident" (69).

The problem with ingesting concentrated amounts of sugar is that the effects are short lived and have consequences. I remember the down side of maintaining my mood with energy boosters that had concentrated carbohydrates and sometimes caffeine. A typical day would consist of having coffee, a donut, lunch, and coke or a candy bar in the afternoon to keep me going.

Arriving home from work I was so irritable I could hardly function. My poor teenage kids were the recipients of my incredibly foul disposition.

Once I took complete control of my diet by obtaining sugars from *complex carbohydrates*, instead of ingesting concentrated pure sucrose, and by including regular portions of protein, I found a profound difference in the way I felt, physically and mentally. The complex carbohydrates are a full package with fiber, vitamins, and minerals, and are metabolized differently and slowly. I also had to include acidophilus and additional fiber in my diet to aid in digestion.

The problem with concentrated sugars is that they contain an unnatural, exorbitant amount of carbohydrates (with none of the associated nutrients) which force the pancreas to excrete too much insulin, a blood-sugar regulating hormone.

The body is always trying to regulate correct blood-sugar levels that determine overall energy levels, disposition, alertness, and the ability to think clearly. When a person's body is unable to regulate the exorbitant amounts of sugar, one of two things happens: the pancreas stops being able to secrete insulin (an exhausted pancreas, as in the case of diabetes) or the pancreas over-produces insulin because it becomes sensitized (resulting in hypoglycemia).

An ex-alcoholic must take responsibility for understanding and appropriating the correct diet. A consistent, nutritious diet is essential to maintaining the biochemical balance of the body and is *another key* to having the ability to drink alcohol moderately. I have absolutely no doubt that it was the combination of my poor diet and inappropriate choices (which enabled me to have an escapist attitude) that culminated in abusive alcohol consumption; moreover, I exacerbated the situation by drinking excessive amounts of alcohol. Again, for ex-alcoholic, moderate drinking, it is *mandatory* to have a consistent, nutritious diet.

Exercise

Information on the benefits of exercise is exhaustive. The consensus is unanimous that exercise is *essential* for a healthy disposition; the body is not meant to be sedentary. You can read magazines and books, watch exercise programs, become educated in the methods and attributes of the different kinds of exercise, and implement a personal program that fits your needs.

One of the hardest parts about exercising is that it isn't any fun at first. You must be result oriented with a realistic, specific goal that represents a level of physical fitness as a target, and realize that obtaining that objective involves the secondary challenge of enjoying the process. Make exercise a habit that is as enjoyable as possible. Committed exercisers or athletes will derive a certain pleasure from pushing themselves beyond their comfort zone. Truly fit, healthy individuals don't pamper themselves. The ex-alcoholic can trade the ability to suffer the anguish of a hangover with the anguish of exercise and become the recipient of the positive consequences. This is in the context of sustaining physical health or appropriate physical development, suited to each individuals needs.

Create a self-image that is physically strong, works hard at being physically strong, and enjoys the rewards of being healthy and strong. From my perspective, it is the professional athletes in competitive sports who provide perfect examples of dedication to physical performance and physical health. Think of yourself as an athlete or an ex-athlete who's maintaining optimum fitness. Model yourself after your favorite athlete psychologically for inspiration. The intention is not to emulate the competitive spirit (unless you want to), but rather to imagine stepping into a stronger body, some model of fitness, for fun and inspiration during your exercise routine.

If the model of athletes from competitive sports doesn't work for you, use whatever model of fitness that you identify with to inspire and motivate you. The objective is to have optimum health: high energy levels, good biochemical balance and circulation from an exercised heart, lungs and muscles. Don't resist exercise. Don't be half-hearted. Be fully committed, obligated, to a repeatable schedule of exercise.

Ex-alcoholics will expect an immediate good feeling if they do something that's good for them – like exercise. They are in the habit of experiencing quickly induced states of euphoria.

Our present culture has an instant gratification psychology with quick and easy to access conveniences. Exercise is often not a quick or easy way to feel better; but, remember that for optimum well-being, one *needs* physical exercise. Be patient and keep returning to an exercise routine that suits your needs. I know several people, as well as myself, who derive pleasure from exercise and look forward to it. It represents a repeatable area of a maturing sense of well-being and control. The positive consequences are numerous, as well as motivating.

Ritual

One aspect of the moderate individual that could be taken for granted, but should not be, is the behavior of ritual. Its importance cannot be overstated. Ritualizing moderate alcohol consumption creates a context for appropriateness and boundaries. It's not necessarily a conscious process, nor always acknowledged as ritual, but healthy individuals ritualize sleeping, eating, brushing their teeth, taking showers, exercising, meditating. The list goes on. The healthy person will anticipate a ritual, will be cognizant of how it complements his or her well-being, and will perform the act ceremoniously. It's not just a habit. It's honoring, respecting, and taking a repeatable, healthy-habit pattern seriously.

The committed obligation to ritual can have a significant effect on behavior. When it represents an *immutable commitment* to very specific boundaries concerning alcohol consumption, ritual alone keeps one from overindulgence. Conversely, alcoholics display flagrant disregard for rituals that are synonymous with a healthy lifestyle. The unhealthy rituals acquired from the abusive alcoholic behavior need to be acknowledged and replaced with healthy-habit patterns, as replacing drinking all night with moderate alcohol consumption and a good night's sleep.

Ex-alcoholics could have a resistance to ritual as a result of their previous habit of unrestrained behavior. But they can acknowledge that the freedom to be uninhibited, carefree and spontaneous works in concert with the freedom to do what they ought. Being carefree and having fun is not in conflict with staying clear headed and sober. Also, ritual does not imply doing something at the same time every day; it could be something done once a week, or once a year at a Christmas get-together. It could be done completely spontaneously. The point is, it's an activity one does with appreciation and respect. It is never used as an opportunity to be indulgent.

There is a possible negative connotation to the term or idea of ritual acquired from the memory of unappreciated obligations, involving churches, schools, family, and other institutions. It is important not to let previous conditioning bother you and to acknowledge the world of your own personal, healthy-habit patterns. There are healthy rituals that you own, you control, and nobody can interfere with. Whether or not you participate in external rituals, as participating in the activities of a church, is optional and up to the discretion or desire of each individual.

If the ex-alcoholic's moderate alcohol consumption is not in some obvious ritual, it will be treated as quasi-ritual; that is, it is always performed in the proper context with appreciation and respect. I know people who regularly drink a glass of wine with dinner. The drink, as well as the dinner itself, is fully appreciated and acknowledged as a complement to their well-being. Form good habits and perform them ceremoniously and with reverence.

Affirmations

Brian Tracy in *The Luck Factor* states, "Whatever strong affirmative statement you repeat over and over in your conscious mind will soon be accepted as command in your subconscious." Tell yourself the same thing every day and eventually you assimilate it; you believe it. This effect of intentionally or unintentionally modifying how one thinks, by constant iteration of a conscious thought or saying, can have profound consequences in behavior.

Realize, also, that constant iteration of a thought and its resulting consequences can work against you. Never tell yourself negative affirmations, as "I am an alcoholic," or you'll believe them. Replace "I am an alcoholic" with "I am a moderate person" or "I have the power not to drink" or "I chose sobriety." If you know that you would still want to overindulge if you drank, and someone asks if you'd like a drink, or asks why you don't drink alcohol, don't say it's because "I am a alcoholic." It's better to say something as, "I avoid alcohol (will not drink alcohol right now) because I still feel like I would want to overindulge." It's wordier but has no negative message, and you understand it's because you would *want* to overindulge. You can also pass on the subject and not answer. Don't feel obligated to explain your personal choices to others if you are so inclined. It does not have to be an issue, but you should know why *you* chose to drink or not drink.

Perhaps if small amounts of alcohol cause you physiological problems, just say, "It doesn't agree with me." Whatever it is, tell it like it is to yourself, and say what you please to others. If you don't understand why you drink uncontrollably, figure it out. Saying "I am an alcoholic" during an AA meeting implies you *inherently* don't have control over alcohol, and because you believe "I will always be an alcoholic," you relinquish the responsibility to honestly figure out why you are overindulgent. Consequently, you hope you will "... live without drinking 'one day at a time,'" and never *accidentally* get drunk.

Look in the mirror and say, "I am a moderate person;" see a moderate person; feel like a moderate person. Some might say, "But I know if I were to start drinking, I wouldn't quit. How can I look in the mirror and honestly say I am a moderate person?" Realize you're programming yourself to be or feel a certain way every time you talk to yourself; therefore, give yourself only positive messages. I'm not suggesting that you tell yourself you're a moderate person and pretend that you can drink alcohol when you know you will overindulge.

Alcoholics wake up in the morning, look in the mirror and can honestly say, "I'm an alcoholic," because they are. Moreover, notice it's a negative message. People who don't drink alcohol and say, "I am a moderate person," are not being dishonest. Even if they presently feel they would overindulge if they drank, and therefore don't drink, they realize moderation in all things (omitting alcohol) is in their best interest.

Think or say only that which is in your best interest. Very methodically list the characteristics of your ideal self and repeat them to yourself every day. Stick with it and make it a habit. Slowly, initially almost indiscernibly, you *will* reap the benefits of this small investment in yourself.

Meditation

Meditation is spiritual introspection or can also be a state of reflection where there is the contemplation of thoughts or external events. The practice of meditation that is applicable to the ex-alcoholic is the intentional, regular, ritualistic activity of sitting quietly for a period of about a half-hour while exercising focused introspection. This activity serves as a reference, a moment of silence, and as a reminder of who one is, including being a moderate person.

I must admit, of all the things I've done in my post-alcoholic lifestyle, meditation has had the most subtle, but most significant, effect. It has been subtle in the fact that there has been no quick or dramatic change in the way I feel, but significant in the way meditation has influenced my behavioral priorities. By placing morning meditations as a priority in my schedule, I knew I wouldn't get drunk at night. That might sound like a stretch, but I distinctly remember, early in my recovery, my behavior at night was effected by the fact I was going to meditate in the morning. I have had the habit of meditating directly after breakfast every day for years. I don't think it's a coincidence that over the same period of time, I have been able to drink moderately.

The procedure I use is the following: Sit comfortably in a quiet room with no distractions (I wear earplugs) and acknowledge pressing concerns; write down concerns, perhaps as questions, then review your affirmations; close your eyes and focus your attention on being as relaxed as you possibly can; count backwards and between numbers, silently tell yourself to relax while observing your breath and/or heartbeat. The priority is to relax physically, concentrate on a thought or a series of specific thoughts, relinquish concern and have a completely passive attitude by just observing, unjudgingly observing.

Meditation is an exercise in being still, relaxed, quiet. It is physical inactivity with a focus on some internal visualization that complements being at peace and living a harmonious lifestyle. Sometimes this exercise can be used to visualize a desired event or self-image. The recovering alcoholic can develop a positive self-image and ascertain a sanctuary of calm from the regular exercise of meditation. The act is not related to any specific religion or philosophy. There are no prerequisites for the practice.

One thing we know about this experience is that it will elicit a healing response because the optimum condition of the body to heal itself is in the relaxed state. In addition, the mind is clear and most creative when it is uninhibited and relaxed; the conscious intention to relax on command is powerful, indeed.

The benefits of regular mediation have become scientifically documented. Herbert Benson in *The Relaxation Response*, provides documentation on the attributes of meditation as being able to relieve tension and stress. There are several books, classes and sources of information on the subject of meditation. Seek them out if you haven't already done so, and develop a habit that will make another significant contribution to your ability to enjoy the freedom of moderation.

Drinking Alcohol

Here's the easy part. I used to drink a beer in fifteen to thirty minutes; now I drink a beer in an hour and a half. Sound hard? It's easy – just sip very slowly; never drink fast. There should never be a significant change in how you feel; you want to *minimize the effects of the alcohol*; and remember, you are not drinking to get drunk, *ever*. A moderate amount of alcohol does not make you drunk, high, dopey or significantly alter your mood. Never drink on an empty stomach or under stress.

I like to frequent bars so I can listen to live music, and I enjoy my evenings of moderation completely. I remember when I was a practicing alcoholic, I used to get blasted and I would anticipate a wild, crazy, frenzied experience where everyone was higher-than-a-kite. Remember, be careful what you ask for; your expectations and what you anticipate become self-fulfilling prophecies. It is the content of your mind that determines the condition of your life.

Never participate in group insanity; always maintain complete aloofness. If you're not participating in some activity, don't hang out or spend long periods of time in environments that serve alcohol. Other than an immutable desire to stay sober, the art of drinking alcohol moderately is dependent on two things: the speed at which you drink, and the amount of time you spend drinking, which represents volume. It's the rate of drinking and the volume of alcohol that one has to be ever cognizant of.

If you're going out and you know you're going to participate in alcohol consumption, anticipate drinking a small amount of alcohol slowly. If you don't feel comfortable spending long periods of time in environments that serve alcohol (sometimes push alcohol), then show up late or leave early; you won't miss anything. Remember the party is with you and the party is the mastery of moderation. This is not a concept; it is a real, consistent, satisfying feeling which once you've experienced, you will never allow to be taken away.

One of the most studied and easy to find aspects of alcohol consumption addresses the effects of specific amounts of alcohol to people of particular weights over certain periods of time. Locally, we have sobriety checks in which the police investigate the drivers in vehicles in an effort to discourage drunk driving. At these sobriety checks the police will hand out an Alcohol Impairment Chart which is intended only as a "guide," describing blood alcohol levels in a table with body weight versus "The Number of Drinks Over a Two Hour Period." This concern over alcohol consumption and its effects are valid.

Small amounts of alcohol can tend to stimulate an individual, but alcohol is a depressant drug and larger amounts of alcohol will depress a person's reasoning and judgment. The depression of reasoning and judgment, combined with euphoria, is the black hole of alcoholism that is to be avoided like the plague. Alcoholics have a propensity to reach the threshold of a depression in reasoning much sooner than other "normal" individuals. It is the depression of reasoning that the ex-alcoholic drinker will *intentionally avoid.*

If you chose to drink alcohol and you have an honest desire to stay sober, you MUST *slowly* drink a *small amount* of alcohol, while ever so cognizantly avoiding the threshold of a depression in reasoning, where one more drink and then just ooonne more drink seem like a "good" idea.

Change "... can't drink just one beer," referring to having to drink several (another saying from AA), to "... just one beer." I've heard that there are people who are very sensitive to small amounts of alcohol, but I personally don't know of anybody who gets drunk or out of control or has some kind of allergic reaction to *slowly* drinking just one drink. I enjoy slowly drinking small quantities of alcohol, and I never want to get drunk. As an ex-alcoholic, I find the sense of satisfaction that is derived from that experience (not wanting to get drunk while drinking alcohol) is more enjoyable than the drink itself. Occasionally, I like to drink a brandy and tea with honey, or perhaps wine with dinner.

One of the considerations of the ex-alcoholic moderate drinker is socializing with others who will drink a generous amount alcohol, then stop drinking before they are drunk. These are the types of individuals who have the opposite disposition to those who have the propensity to uncontrollably drink exorbitant amounts of alcohol. NEVER match the drinking style of someone else. NEVER be persuaded to "join in," as a friendly gesture, to slam a quick one, or have one more. NEVER anticipate or expect that you can drink like someone else. Be completely independent, inflexible, immovable on the matter of moderation with alcohol. It is the adamant, immutable desire to stay sober, combined with intentionally avoiding the threshold of a depression in reasoning, that enables the ex-alcoholic moderate drinker to slowly drink a small amount of alcohol or none at all.

Don't feel obligated to finish alcoholic drinks in relation to dictated volumes, as the 6 oz glass of wine, or 12 oz bottle of beer, the full shot of liquor. Sometimes I find just one ounce (approximately) of wine with a meal is quite satisfying. Don't finish a beer if you don't feel like it. Give yourself permission to have *small* amounts of alcohol, even if it's just a couple sips for taste. Moderation is the key.

There is the question of the party that lasts for hours. How do you have just one drink if the occasion lasts all day? An occasion is never just about alcohol; if it is, you don't belong there. Remember, use one drink every one and a half to two hours, depending on your weight, with food in between as a "guide." Don't drink just alcohol; drink juice, water, or coffee. Remember you are enjoying moderation at a social event and *avoiding* the feeling of being tipsy. This is not a concept you have to remind yourself of, it is an *honest desire to stay clear-headed and sober.*

There is the argument that someday, because I drink and hang out in environments that serve alcohol, I may be more tempted or could somehow get carried away in the moment; I might accidentally overindulge and go right back to being an alcoholic. If you share that concern, let me make this very clear. There is no such thing as an accident – ever. All things happen by law and that law is the content of your mind. You cannot even remotely be tempted to be overindulgent, unless you *previously* thought of it as a good idea, or as pleasurable. You have to give yourself permission, or view it as a curiosity, ahead of time.

Ask yourself, back when you were a practicing alcoholic, how many times did you start the first drink and know you were going to get drunk? Or suspected....? Or said to yourself, "I'll only have a couple." The answer is invariably always. You will *always* know ahead of time if you will get drunk. That foreknowledge, an ambiguous desire perhaps, is the predisposition to disaster. Even if you don't want to get drunk because you might have an important engagement the following day and you just want a little to unwind, you'll probably overindulge. Why? Because even though you don't have the forethought, "I'm going to get drunk," you always have the intention to change how you feel. A little intention becomes liberal.

Also, you drink alcoholically; that is, you drink fast. Drinking fast (as well as a large quantity) is how alcoholics reach a depression in reasoning. Because you historically tend to overindulge, you know that you might again; you doubt. The option to get drunk is always there because at some point, perhaps after a couple drinks, being intoxicated is viewed as a pleasurable thing to be.

Moderate drinkers *never* think of being drunk as an option. They *never want* to get "high." They detest intoxication, are repelled by it. There is *never* the slightest intention to overindulge. Getting intoxicated is out of the question because they *believe* it is undesirable, and there is *never any doubt*.

I repeat, unless you have thought of being drunk as a good idea or as pleasurable, you will not overindulge. Before you are able to become intoxicated, you have to previously consider, entertain, or have some type of curiosity about being under the influence of alcohol.

Ask yourself the question, "Who's more likely to get drunk under tempting circumstances – the ex-alcoholic who is the personification of moderation, or the individual who, because of his/her association with a rehabilitation organization, repeats to themselves on a regular basis 'I am an alcoholic?'" Alcoholics are so used to being out of control, it's hard for them to believe that someone who has had a history of overindulgence can have complete freedom, even to have a drink in a bar, and not want to get drunk. Moderate individuals not only lack the desire to get drunk, they are cognizant of their surroundings, and anticipate and avoid any situation that is undesirable.

Your life is not about alcohol – moderation is freedom from alcohol abuse. Freedom from alcohol abuse is *never* to have a hangover. Non-practicing alcoholics say the motto

"...live without drinking 'one day at a time'," which is indicative of their inability to trust themselves not to get drunk, from one day to the next. They don't realize there is an immutable foundation in *knowing* "I am a moderate person" that can free one from fear and doubt.

Remember, one has to abolish completely, without reservation, all thoughts or feelings of being inebriated as fun or pleasurable. Don't just disassociate pleasure with intoxication using the easy points like the hangovers, the belligerence, or lack of control, but also remove any association of pleasure from the most desirable aspect – being high. Loathe *all* the stages of overindulgence: the initial onset of being tipsy, the high, the drunk, the consequences. Never think of feeling good as being high.

Cigarettes

Just briefly, I will mention cigarettes, an unhealthy and addictive habit. Cigarette smoking is very common among overindulgent, self-abusive personalities, like alcoholics. Habitual smoking is a perfect example of an anticipating gratification cycle representing a dependence on a substance that is unhealthy. It is the habit of needing a fix with a smoke to maintain your disposition that can nurse and maintain a gratification cycle, which at a different time can represent drinking too much alcohol. Remember, the enjoyable cycles of a healthy lifestyle do not involve mood maintenance fixes by using unhealthy substances and/or overindulgence.

Recently, the tobacco industry has incurred more liability for smoking-related illnesses. It's interesting that neither warning labels nor the observation of people suffering from tobacco-related illnesses doesn't deter more people from smoking. Inhaling a cocktail of chemicals, as the result of burning tobacco laced with other substances, none of which are nutrients for the body, is an abomination. I have watched several people suffer and die prematurely from cigarette-related illnesses.

Why do people smoke? Because they think it's pleasurable. List all the reasons why cigarettes are *not* pleasurable, including being a slave to the tobacco industry. Think of everything, as the knowledge that it clogs your lungs and the residual left in your mouth. Notice that some of the time you don't really enjoy smoking. You actually treat it like a nuisance because you intuitively know it's a bad habit. Paradoxically, I've heard it said, "It's because I have the right to enjoy myself; it's my little treat to myself."

Treat yourself to the pleasure of not smoking. Think of yourself as a non-smoker. Catch yourself identifying with others you see smoking, and consciously stop the thought. Don't identify with the image of being a smoker.

Create the objective to be a non-smoker as an enjoyable experience. Visualize yourself enjoying being a non-smoker. Repeat the affirmation, "I am a non-smoker," over and over. Feel it, think it, and it will be you. Convince yourself that cigarettes are not pleasurable and your actions will follow. It will take no willpower because you will not *want* to smoke.

The Action of Moderation, Key Points:

• Food effects our physical and mental dispositions. A consistent nutritious diet is mandatory.

• Exercise is essential for a healthy disposition.

• Ritual is a fundamental aspect of a healthy individual: good habits performed ceremoniously and with respect.

• Affirmations effect behavior. Repeat only nurturing statements to yourself.

• Meditation promotes relaxation and self-image modification.

• Moderation is drinking a small amount of alcohol slowly.

• Cigarettes are unhealthy and addictive. Repeat, "I am a non-smoker." Feel it; think it over and over to quit smoking.

Chapter 8

The Feeling of Moderation

Not Enough to What Is

The crux of the whole issue around addictive behavior is that it is all about how one feels. The way a person feels precedes, resides within, and follows all action. It is the greatest motivator. It is the essence of identity: how one feels. The underlying desire to feel good is a basic premise to all life, so the question is: why do so many people indulge in destructive behavior?

The answer is twofold. It is both the psychological and biochemical dispositions that determine how one feels. Each influences the other, but they can be viewed as independent factors. This is where genetic influences and conditioning come into play, and provide the foundation or propensity to be an alcoholic or a substance abuser. The propensity to be an alcoholic provides the basis of the victim psychology that states, "I am powerless over alcohol," or "once an alcoholic, always an alcoholic."

One common experience of all addicts and potential addicts, the people with the propensity to "use and abuse," is that they don't feel as if they are enough. Perhaps they did not receive unconditional love when they were young, or their genetic dispositions provide a biochemical imbalance. The feeling of inadequacy is always experienced as, "I don't feel as if I am enough." Frequently, people with the propensity to be overindulgent wake up in the morning and have the distinct feeling that they're missing something. The cause of that feeling could be displaced by an attempt to understand it, be it, "I don't have companionship," or "I don't make enough money." The feeling of "not enough" or "missing something" is blamed on something else out there, but the experience is always felt as an internal discontent or dissatisfaction.

When an alcoholic is drinking, he/she will trade the feeling of missing something to being onto something – on the verge of some kind of enlightenment or emotional well-being. I remember the very distinct feeling, while intoxicated, that I was onto something, "I'm almost there, just one more beer." I felt compelled to get drunk; I *had* to overindulge or I would be missing out on something important.

It was because of a combination of arbitrary, mental conditioning and body chemistry that I was able to walk down the path of alcoholism. I felt I had no alternatives but to rebel against the "system" (be a dropout hippie with no responsibilities), which led to an escapist attitude and a lifestyle of corrupted values and terrible diet. I have the genetic propensity to have low blood sugar (hypoglycemia) and exacerbated the problem by drinking coke, excessive amounts of coffee, and, of course, during my alcoholic years, drinking dangerous amounts of alcohol. I completely exhausted my endocrine system (which regulates sleep to alertness, and the body's blood sugar level). Because I had the tendency to have low blood sugar, I would compensate with huge extremes in intoxication. My poor body became conditioned to expect and anticipate the next high to escape the present low. The question was, "How do I stop this cycle of defeat?"

In the previous chapters I have provided the workings of how one can be independent from substance abuse; however, all efforts will fail the goal of immutable sobriety if one does not come to terms with how he/she feels. The most crucial point is that if you don't feel good, don't think of it as something bad that can be changed by altering your body chemistry with alcohol or some exotic drug. Feeling bad is OK. Sometimes feeling bad will occur, and when it does, don't try to change it with drugs. There are numerous, legitimate reasons why an individual will occasionally experience physical or psychological pain. One of the problems with the abusive personality is he/she is in the habit of inappropriately experiencing physical and psychological pain.

The recovering individuals need to try and understand their pain by asking the question, "Why do I feel bad?" Diagnosis is half the cure. Try to notice whether it is the result of a lack of sleep or too much sleep, your last meal or lack of it, a house full of noisy kids, or perhaps the content of your mind. Write the answers, then ask the questions, "How much control do I have over this? What can I do to alleviate or minimize this problem?" The objective is to confidently conjure up as much control over the situation as possible.

Once you know why you don't feel good, you can work on a change. How you feel will not change immediately, as with drugs or alcohol, but you have the information about yourself to acquire an appropriate long-term solution. Accept "what is" while you work on what you'd like it to be. Intentionally avoid the alcoholic behavior of relinquishing control (to alcohol) and having the negative expectation that problems cannot be resolved.

Another key point is not to be in a hurry, even if you know why you feel bad. Invariably the situation will not go away immediately. Realize the feeling is temporary and appropriate behavior is the only long-term solution. While you're taking appropriate action, just experience what it is to feel lonely or irritable, or whatever discomfort it may be. Even if you're confused, never think of escaping a bad feeling with alcohol or drugs.

From the alcoholic's perspective there is the concern that not wanting to get drunk when you feel bad is easier said than done. There is the repeatable, overwhelming desire to compensate for an uncomfortable feeling. But that perspective is true only because feeling bad is not OK. In order to be free of addictive behavior, you have to acknowledge that *feeling bad is OK.* Feeling bad is OK. Say it over and over again until it makes sense. Acceptance of uncomfortable feelings while working on an appropriate long-term solution is one of the *keys* to post alcoholic moderate drinking.

Feeling bad periodically happens to everybody; it's how you *react* to emotional or physical pain that characterizes you as a stable or unstable personality. Life has its share of hard knocks and if you willingly experience the pain while participating in a solution, the painful situation will pass. If, on the other hand, you chose to alleviate the discomfort by getting high, you will never appropriately resolve the cause of the uncomfortable feeling.

Alcoholics are under the impression that life is meant to be easy and full of enjoyable experiences, and because life is periodically difficult and uncomfortable, they deserve to get high. After all, "It's only right that I feel good" is the internal refrain. In that they are correct. It's right for everyone to expect that they should feel good; however, the experience of well-being can only be built on the consistent and completely satisfying lifestyle of moderation.

Even when things get crazy or painful, that experience will be superimposed with the experience of your personal integrity and your identity as a moderate person. You will know that getting drunk is not an option. No more extreme highs or extreme lows, there will only be the consistent, repeatable attributes of moderation.

Realize you will feel terrible at first as you wean yourself from an abusive lifestyle. Your body could be imbalanced and in a state of recovery for a relatively long time. There is no doubt about it – you *will* feel bad. The painful void that precedes negative behavior can be horrendous. That is why you have to come to terms with the uncomfortable aspects of rehabilitation.

Try to distract yourself with something that is good for you, like a hot bath or cup of tea. Don't personalize the experience. Initiate a self-image that is highly motivated and preoccupied with things that are more important than post-alcoholic suffering. Trade your ability to "tough out" a hangover with the ability to "tough out" staying sober. Notice the cravings are absent. Take pleasure in the sense of control. Be patient.

When I knew I could weather any emotional or physical discomfort, like loneliness or low blood sugar, without *want-*

ing to escape with alcohol, I knew I had alcoholism licked. I cannot pretend that this was easy. At first, the periods I spent in confusion from biochemical imbalances combined with post alcoholic shame were truly mind-boggling. But, I didn't want to get drunk because I didn't associate pleasure with it anymore. I just wanted my life back, and I knew that however I felt was temporary.

Biochemical Machines

We are biochemical machines. Everything we put in our body for sustenance is a chemical and will have an effect on our biochemical disposition. Appropriate substances in food and drink are one of the ways we regulate our well-being. You have to eat and drink appropriate substances moderately to feel good.

Moderation in all things implies only appropriate substances. Our culture is full of substances that should not even be options and I will not make an issue of their legality, only the appropriateness of their effects. For example, it is never appropriate behavior to smoke pot or use cocaine recreationally. Perhaps, this may be a point of contention for some, especially occasional users who haven't experienced deterioration in the quality of their lives as a direct result of what is known as recreational drug use. But, consider the facts: when you participate in using drugs that make you "feel good," you will experience a quickly exaggerated amount of endorphins released, producing an illusion that all is well.

This quickly exaggerated high is exactly what moderate individuals *intentionally avoid.* The exorbitant amount of quickly induced endorphins set up the body and mind to rush into amplified states of feeling. This physical and mental destabilizing experience opens the floodgates for disregard of control, reservation, and the ability to stay calm, as if the body has an agenda or mind of its own. This condition, once trained into the mind/body system, will exhibit itself inappropriately throughout the course of any day at any time, subsequent to regular drug abuse. The mind/body will jump into unwarranted, heightened states of emotion instantly. Perhaps low blood sugar or stress at work will trigger it, but repeated exaggerated states of euphoria with subsequent lows, *train* the body and mind to be unstable.

Another fundamental problem with mood-enhancing drugs is that they are immediately addictive, not necessarily in a physical sense, but always in a psychological one. For regular drug abuse, physical and psychological addiction is an easily observable consequence. Occasional recreational drug users can acknowledge they become conditioned to anticipate occasions with the enhancement from a drug, and will feel let down or not want to participate in an activity without the use of the drug.

For the ex-alcoholic, the use of drugs, whether for recreational mood-enhancement or for escaping bad feelings, has to be realized as undermining and inappropriate behavior. We are physically and psychologically dependent on good food, healthy habits, satisfying relationships, a sense of purpose, and a safe environment. If we compensate for the absence of any of those needs by using a mood-enhancing drug, our bodies will immediately perceive the drug as a need. Not feeling good is a healthy feedback mechanism communicating that something is not right; however, if compensating for an undesirable feeling represents using unhealthy substances and/or overindulgence, you mask the initial problem and exacerbate the situation with substance abuse.

By appropriately dealing with the cause of an undesirable sensation, you will minimize it or it will not reoccur. If you take a drug to deal with an unpleasant experience, it will forever and consistently reoccur. The fundamental cause is never resolved; and, when the mind says, "In order to feel good, I take this drug," you're hooked.

Thought Control

Trying to understand why you don't feel good, whether it is a general level of dissatisfaction or more specific pain, can be a daunting task for a rehabilitating alcoholic. In retrospect, it might seem evident, but alcoholics have everything muddled into a ball of confusion and pain. Once you realize you can enjoy life without addictive behavior and without forced willpower, just by adamantly wanting to be moderate, you can start to sort through the mess.

Other than dealing with the physical contributions to your disposition, diet and exercise, you have to acknowledge the consequences of your thoughts. This could sound like a redundant theme, but I'm specifically addressing the emotional content or *feelings* of being a moderate person as a consequence of internal dialogue. The abusive behavior of living the wrong lifestyle can destroy your physical condition and, subsequently, the way you feel; but, it is not always so apparent that your thoughts have everything to do with how you feel.

If an alcoholic feels that he/she is a victim, the ensuing uncomfortable experience is the direct result of this thought. Whether or not it is based on fact is irrelevant. Acknowledge when you feel bad because of a thought, a thought that you choose to think and is causing you to feel bad. Your victim psychology will defend its position by saying, "I have to think about it; this is what my life is all about."

It is not the details in the dilemma that will necessarily affect you, but the context or attitude will, the "I am a victim (context) because of ... (details)." Destroy the negative contextual attitude (victim thought pattern) and the details will take care of themselves, or at least be seen in a different light. Remember, what you think becomes your reality. As James Allen says in *As A Man Thinketh*, "The outer world of circumstance shapes itself to the inner world of thought" (11).

Ask the question, "What's good in my life?" At first the answer could be, "Nothing," or "Not much," and that will be the point. If you are inclined to think of yourself as a victim, you have a habit of noticing, entertaining and worrying about your problems so much, you're miserable.

The unencumbered lifestyle of those who are more often than not content and happy is not an accident. They're happy because they intentionally search for the good. Search for the good, and always have the positive expectation that the solutions to your problems are imminent.

Why Be Sober?

Alcoholics, people with abusive lifestyles, wake up with incredible hangovers and wonder why they're alive, as if some purpose or intent is slipping through their fingers. A gloomy, "How much longer can I go on like this?" is the question that starts the day. At this juncture alcoholics are no longer in denial and have a strong desire to have freedom from alcohol overindulgence, but are still ambivalent, and amazingly enough, still don't consider sobriety an appealing alternative.

They will concede they need a strong, incredibly convincing psychological antidote to alcohol.

Other than the disruption and suffering associated with alcoholism, what compelling aspect of being sober will motivate an individual to drink moderately? What will be satisfying enough for that individual to stay sober? Somehow, he/she has to be completely convinced that the lifestyle of a moderate, sober individual is significantly, immeasurably more enjoyable and satisfying than the lifestyle of an alcoholic.

The question, "What could motivate me to stay sober?" if not answered adequately, will send the unsuspecting, rehabilitating alcoholic right back to being a practicing alcoholic. Everything associated with diet or any activity, like exercise or work, is to complement the *need* to feel good. Otherwise, through intoxication, the alcoholic could participate in an inappropriate compensation for the lack of a sense of well-being.

Everyone is always motivated by the *desire to experience a sense of well-being*. This acknowledgment is the fundamental, bedrock foundation of understanding that will enable an individual to get sober and stay sober. Once an alcoholic *understands* that being in exaggerated states of inebriation and that having fun by being blasted are not synonymous with the satisfying feelings that can be found in moderation, they start to see the light. In order to feel *really good* you have to stay sober, eat right, sleep right, exercise, have positive thought patterns and affirmations, and meditate. Invariably, this represents hard work and sometimes it's not easy.

Notice that having fun or feeling good is a consequence of going about the business of being what you ought to be, and doing what you ought to do. Understand that if your happiness comes from a drug, you will need the drug to be happy. The alcoholic can be motivated to be straight, even to be a moderate drinker, if he/she understands the objective is to feel good, as in having peace of mind, contentment, truly satisfying feelings of well-being. Once understood, this satisfying feeling is what everyone wants; it is truly motivating and becomes an inalienable reason to stay sober.

Control of Action versus Control of Feeling

Early in my recovery it became evident that the rate of recovery in relation to control of my actions was different from the rate of recovery in relation to control of how I felt. I recall a definite difference in my ability to eat right, exercise, and drink moderately (action), as opposed to not feeling shame and remorse (feelings). It is necessary to make the critical distinction between action and feeling.

Somehow, I programmed myself so thoroughly while waking, in those initial moments of consciousness, I would make statements, as "You are disgusting; I hate you." Consequently, feeling bad was still there after the abusive behavior was long gone. That is, the shame and remorse and low self-esteem followed me around even when I wasn't doing anything to deserve it (conditioned response no longer based on reality).

The point is, recovery is a mixed bag of different aspects of one's life, and improvements take place at different rates. Be patient and don't be discouraged by certain aspects of your life not returning to "normal" as fast as others. Most importantly, never compromise your actions by getting drunk because of a persistent or hard-to-control *feeling*.

The ability to have a sense of well-being is a complex combination of a person's genetic propensity and primary conditioning. The only chance an adult has to improve his/her sense of well-being and self-esteem is to pursue behavior modification by applying appropriate thought and action with detailed attention to (I repeat) values, reference group, attitude, diet, exercise, rituals, affirmations, and meditation.

The Feeling of Moderation, Key Points:

- Desire for a sense of well-being is a basic premise to life.

- Alcohol cannot adequately satisfy the feeling of inadequacy.

- Appropriate long-term solutions need an acceptance of "what is" while problems are being worked out.

- Drugs cause exaggerated states, which moderation *intentionally avoids.*

- Drugs are physically and mentally destabilizing. Drugs are addictive.

- Thought affects how you feel. Remove victim psychology and other negative thought patterns.

- Sobriety enables the objective to have truly satisfying feelings of well-being.

- Different aspects of one's life improve at different rates. Be patient with recovery.

Chapter 9

About God and an Underlying Principle

Middle Ground

There could hardly be a discourse on substance abuse without further mention on the subject of God. Early in recovery programs is the admonition to surrender to a "Power greater than ourselves." In the *Twelve Steps and Twelve Traditions* of Alcoholics Anonymous, six of the steps make direct reference to God. To the recovering alcoholic, moral inventory and contemplation on the meaning of life and the meaning of God typically feels appropriate. There is the fresh memory of being completely humiliated by uncontrollably ingesting exorbitant amounts of alcohol and being completely out of control, thereby creating a desire for help, all the help one can get. If the suffering alcoholic believes in God, or even suspects there is a God, then Divine intervention will be perceived as necessary.

How well this works is always contingent on the level of belief. If an individual believes that God is primarily benevolent, then God becomes the *ultimate* reference of that which is good. The more people believe in the attributes of God, which represent an internal reference of specific ethical characteristics, the more influence these beliefs will have in their lives. Even though occasionally the concept of God might seem confusing and slightly ambiguous, recovering alcoholics can gleam behavior modification proportionally to what they believe. It is the content of what recovering alcoholics believe (including mandatory adherence to moral conduct), as well as the intensity of belief, that can have a significant influence on their rehabilitation.

This approach presumes ethics and morality are the results of a religious affiliation or that the conscience is emanating from a Divine Source. Modern empirical methods which question religious beliefs or the omniscience of a Higher Power point out that ethics and morality are not absent in agnostics and atheists. Ethics and morality can be derived from parents, culture or a religious affiliation, and the source of ethical behavior becomes irrelevant to the result, including moderation.

However, for the believer there is an objective to go beyond ethics and morality and search out the spiritual aspects of life. It is the belief in a Higher Power that can enable an individual to more readily acquire a sense of well-being, as a result of feeling forgiven by Heavenly Powers. This subjective, cathartic experience – feeling forgiven, loved and wanted – creates a sense of self-worth that is not so easily acquired from the self (who omits a Higher Power) or external sources, like parents or culture, especially after habitual, abusive alcohol consumption.

If one is inclined to contemplate the meaning of God, one thing is certain: the realization of any spiritual attainment will only occur through the practice of a lifestyle of moderation or abstinence. Alcoholics might feel like they are having a spiritual experience while in some euphoric state of intoxication; but they will, unfortunately, be farther than ever from the subtleties of spiritual peace.

Though the existence of God may be unsubstantiated, I know it was the direct result of my desire to acquire an understanding of Divine principles that played a significant role in my ability to be an ex-alcoholic, moderate drinker. This search led me to an understanding and an appreciation of Divinity that was quite different from the concepts I acquired from my parochial school background.

The search for truth reveals a curious paradox, where on one side healthy doubt or honest inquisitiveness can provide questions, as "How do I know this is real or appropriate?" and can enable an individual to disengage from inappropriate associations, as by disassociating from a particular pseudo-science or prohibitive, religious dogma. However, on the other side of this paradox, utmost doubt, pure skepticism resulting in atheism, is not open to the possibility that Divine intervention is responsible for the tranquillity experienced by those who claim their peace is derived from a Divine Source. Somewhere between the absence of healthy curiosity and skepticism, there is a relevant, middle ground position, where those who search for the truth, concerning physical and spiritual well-being, reside.

Taking this middle ground position frequently becomes an objective for recovering individuals because they are compelled to thoroughly disassociate themselves from their previous indulgent behavior. Consequently, acquiring spiritual awareness can introduce them to being open-minded and being open to instruction, and lead recovering alcoholics to *reconsider* their past beliefs, not just build on them.

If you want to know the full gamut of what you ought, which might include not just being a moderate drinker but having a responsible approach to Divinity, you will need independent study, not just prayer and meditation. It will require analytical inquiries into the nature of Divinity, perhaps even questions like, "What do all religions have in common?" or "How are religions dissimilar?"

Questions of this nature reveal our biases and help us become more aware of our religious conditioning and its effects. A detached, open-minded, broad reaching view of religion removes prejudice, animosity and self-centeredness, while minimizing religious conflict that, conversely, could provide another excuse for the abusive personality to be discontent.

If you believe you will be accountable for your life, as all religions teach, that belief represents a present moment responsibility to be independently accountable. Listen to the convictions of your inner voice and what you know to be true; resist feeling obligated to participate in exclusive ideologies. Minimize the effects of a religious affiliation if you do not feel it is in your best interest.

Underlying Principle
Acknowledging the consequences of our internal world is the underlying principle of mental causation. We are all, independently, the recipients of our inner-most thoughts and

desires. This principle has been previously mentioned, but because it provides the basis for moderation, it deserves individual attention.

Causative activity is the content of the mind. Mental activity – beliefs, desires, intentions – have causal effects on our circumstances. The statement, the content of your mind is cause and your circumstances are effect, asserts that what you think about has everything to do with the conditions in your life. We are all participating in our own self-fulfilling prophecies with what we choose to contemplate, worry about, or desire. How we act or react is always contingent on mental activity; that is, beliefs desires, intentions, biases, prejudices.

A thought *precedes* the consequences or conditions in a person's life. An understanding of this principle can motivate an individual to eliminate entertaining any thoughts of being inebriated. This is where moderation or alcoholism starts – behavior is largely initiated from beliefs, desires and intentions (mental causation). It is the successful modification of the mental activities, incorporating a person's beliefs, desires and intentions, which will enable them to be an ex-alcoholic, moderate drinker.

Being the recipient of our mental activity is metaphorically stated in *As A Man Thinketh*, when James Allen elaborates, "Every thought seed sown or allowed to fall into the mind, and to take root there, produces its own, blossoming sooner or later into act, and bearing its own fruitage of opportunity and circumstance. Good thoughts bear good fruit, bad thoughts bad fruit" (10-11). There are also the consequences of one's thoughts that are not intentionally positive; that is, negative thoughts can come by default. Therefore, one has to *intentionally plant flowers or weeds will grow.*

The effect of mental causality that is deserving of attention for the recovering alcoholic is the consequence of conditioned responses. A person's disposition is frequently dependent on how he/she accepts, rejects, judges, stereotypes, or prejudges. The fact that you will always be the recipient of your evaluation of the content of your awareness has a strong connection to the influences of your previous conditioning. It is always the person making a judgment (as a result of previous conditioning) who *owns* the perception of judgment, and, also, *experiences* the feelings of hatred or love, whatever the case may be.

In another reference that addresses our circumstances as the result of our beliefs, Maxwell Maltz in *Psycho-Cybernetics*, convincingly makes the point that "... our actions, feelings and behavior are the result of our own images and beliefs" (31). Our brain and nervous system react to belief as the causative agent; what you believe to be true is what is real, whether it is based on objective reality or not.

Beliefs are the content of the self-image. This is why it is so important to acknowledge the power of affirmations (repetition of self-nurturing statements). With emotional conviction use affirmations, as "I am a moderate person," on a regular basis, and you will believe them. Believe life is good. Believe you are an unquestionably moderate person. Know that one does not act in a manner that is inconsistent with one's beliefs. What you believe is what you are. The mastery of moderation provides the foundation for spiritual and physical well-being; all personal attributes and skills will flourish only from a *belief* in an identity of being a moderate person.

If you are inclined to be overindulgent and self-destructive, your behavior is the result of genetic propensity augmented with mental content that gives you *permission* to be abusive. Reconsidering the content of your mind, beliefs, desires, intentions, biases, and prejudice is an essential exercise for the rehabilitating alcoholic.

About God and an Underlying Principle, Key Points:

- The content and intensity of a belief in God can influence rehabilitation.

- The balance between the absence of a healthy curiosity and skepticism resides in a relevant, middle ground position.

- The reconsideration of previous beliefs about God requires independent study, not just prayer and meditation.

- The underlying principle of mental causation states that we are all recipients of our beliefs, desires, intentions, biases, and prejudices.

- The content of your mind is cause and your circumstances are the effect.

- The deliberate acquisition of positive thoughts is very important. Intentionally plant flowers or weeds will grow.

- The influences of your previous conditioning, resulting in stereotyping and prejudice, can effect your disposition.

- The content of the self-image is dependent on your beliefs. Believe you are an unquestionably moderate person.

Chapter 10

All Persons Know for Themselves

Occasional Overindulgence

The focus of this book has been primarily about people who drink alcohol uncontrollably on a regular basis; the miserable, the unquestionable alcoholic. In closing I will address the potential alcoholic or occasional drunk once again – those who drink an immoderate amount of alcohol occasionally, just to have fun, the celebrators, the happy drunks. If you want to get drunk, you will. If you think you might get drunk, you will. Happy drunk or unhappy drunk, it doesn't matter. Drunk is drunk, and drunk is disgusting and shameful, not as in judging the behavior of others, but of yours. Whether or not one can be happy without alcohol is the question. Remember, all alcoholics start by being occasional drunks and start by having fun.

Again, one of the characteristics of developing alcoholics is denial. They deny they actually need alcohol to have fun, or they deny they really look forward to the next opportunity when they know they can get high. The developing alcoholics will deny that the overindulgence of alcohol has affected their relationships negatively. They spend a significant amount of time suffering from hangovers, suggesting to themselves that they should be tougher. The biochemistry of the body becomes subliminally locked in to a dependency on alcohol to feel good. The negative thought patterns mature and denial becomes irrational. It is very common for the guilt and shame to rise to intolerable levels before the suffering alcoholic will actually admit to having a problem with alcohol.

The question becomes: How can developing alcoholics be motivated to live moderate lifestyles and avoid years of suffering and denial? They can start by understanding that when people overindulge, they have given themselves permission to do so with all the excuses to have fun, not to take life too seriously, to celebrate, to get away from it all. They are masking their inadequacies and inability to enjoy life without alcohol. The subsequent consequences, resulting hangovers and remorse, create a cycle of dependency where there is the need to escape the suffering, where just a little to unwind becomes an exorbitant amount of alcohol.

STOP the cycle of defeat by having a *strong desire* to be moderate. Make the desire to be moderate a well-defined goal with detailed specifics. Acknowledge that overindulgence is not in your best interest. From experience, LIST every single aspect of overindulgence as such an undesirable prospect that you loathe the thought of intoxication. Through visualization, LIST every single desirable aspect of experiencing a lifestyle of moderation. Once understood and applied, moderation will permeate a sense of well-being in all areas of your life.

If you have the propensity to be an alcoholic, and don't go through the exercise of finding inebriation unpleasant and moderation desirable, you *will* get drunk again. All necessary and complementary suggestions in this book will be built on and centered around finding inebriation unpleasant and moderation desirable.

Knowledge is Not Knowing

It is absolutely imperative that any individual who is entertaining the idea that he/she can be an ex-alcoholic, moderate drinker completely understand this point: A person can have all the applicable *knowledge* on the subject of moderation, but still not *know* they can drink moderately. Again, a person can read this book and several others like it, memorize the material, and still not *know* that they can drink moderately. It is the most defining point I can make in this book. If you have doubt, you will fail.

Understand that knowing you can drink moderately is a discernible *feeling*, a clear indisputable, beyond-the-shadow-of-a-doubt knowing. Don't pretend that the knowledge of this book or any other reference is permission to drink. It is not. Only you know whether or not you are a moderate person. Do not be encouraged or persuaded by other sources on this issue. Only you are responsible for your actions. This is the kind of thing you cannot practice and make mistakes learning. Don't experiment or try and see. There is no such thing as an accident. You either know you can drink moderately, or you don't. If you don't know you can drink alcohol moderately, then don't drink.

If you are inclined to get away from it all, or just want to have fun by using alcohol as a means to that end, then that is a clear indicator that you are not a moderate person. The moderate ex-alcoholic has replaced the desire to be "high" with the desire to be moderate. Again, that discernible feeling is a clear, indisputable, beyond-the-shadow-of-a-doubt knowing.

Autonomy for Everyone

It was my intention to share with others how I have been able to be a moderate person after suffering years of alcoholism. I don't know if I'll ever be satisfied with the way I've presented the information, but it is my hope that those interested in freedom from alcohol addiction will benefit from the content of this effort. They will need to scrutinize their own stories and set specific priorities to accommodate their individual needs. This is a hands-on project that demands personal attention every step of the way. This book is surrounded by someone else's story. It is not a definitive conclusion to all post-alcoholic behavior, but is intended to help point the way. Each person has to take full responsibility for his/her own life.

In reference to moderation, there can be no half-hearted effort. In terms of commitment to moderation, it is for the duration, the rest of your life. To understand your own behavior regarding why you used to overindulge and now you don't, leave no stone unturned. You have to be adamantly, thoroughly committed to moderation.

Feel the excitement of moderation. Experience the confidence of moderation. Anticipate the good. Expect the best. Capture the initial subtle feeling of satisfaction and nurture it. Worship moderation and you will have only the will to be moderate. Behold contentment in moderation. Acknowledge the freedom in moderation. Declare your independence in moderation. Notice there is never an occasion for doubt. Keep a constant vigil.

All Persons Know for Themselves, Key Points:

- Alcoholism starts by being an occasional drunk having fun.

- Moderation must start with finding inebriation unpleasant and moderation desirable.

- Knowledge that you can drink moderately must be beyond-the-shadow-of-a-doubt, or don't drink.

- Moderation must be an unquestionably adamant, desirable, thorough commitment.

References

Alcoholics Anonymous (*the Big Book*), Third Edition, Alcoholics Anonymous World Services, Inc., 1976: 33.

Allen, James. *As A Man Thinketh*, Barnes and Noble, 1992: 2, 11.

Benson, Herbert. *The Relaxation Response*, Avon Books, 1976.

Csikszentmihalyi, Mihaly. *Finding Flow*, BasicBooks, 1997: 122.

Department Of Health And Human Services. *National Household Survey On Drug Abuse Main Findings* 1995, Office of Applied Studies, SAMHSA, 1995: 87.

DesMaisons, Kathleen. *Potatoes Not Prozac*, Simon and Schuster, 1998: 68-69.

Maltz, Maxwell. *Psycho-Cybernetics*, Wilshire Book Company, 1971: XIX, 31.

Raloff, J. "Which is healthier, the wining or dining?" *Science News*, Vol. 155, January 23, 1999: 53.

Robbins, Anthony. *Personal Power Program For Unlimited Success*, Robbins Research International, Inc. 1993.

Twelve Steps and Twelve Traditions, Alcoholics Anonymous World Services, Inc., 1953.

Tracy, Brian. *The Luck Factor*, Nightingale-Conant Corp.

_____. *Psychology of Achievement*, Nightingale-Conant Corp.

Ask your local bookstore to order a copy of *The Art of Moderation: An Alternative to Alcoholism* by John Michael or you may order directly from the publisher.

To order copies directly from VBI by mail use this order form:

      Number of hard cover books ISBN 1-56550-083-0

                    ____ at $14.00 per book $_____

      Number of soft cover books ISBN 1-56550-084-9

                    ____ at $10.00 per book $_____

Sales tax of 7.25% applies to books mailed to California addresses only:

      Number of hard cover books: ____ at $1.02 per book $_____

      Number of soft cover books:____ at $0.73 per book $_____

Shipping and handling at $3.50 for first book (add $2 for each additional book)

                    _____books $_____

                    Total amount enclosed $_____

Name:_____

Mailing address:_____

City:_____State:_____Zip_____

Please send a check or money order (no cash or C.O.D.) to:
Vision Books International
PMB 342
775 East Blithedale Avenue
Mill Valley, CA 94941

John Michael may be contacted by e-mail at jmike@sonic.net for further discussion.